The Understanding of Good

Thoughts on Some of Life's Higher Issues

Jeanne de Vietinghoff

Translated by
Ethel Ireland Helleman

Edited and Introduced by
Christine Mary McGinley

Gleam of Light Press
U.S.A.

The Understanding of Good:
Thoughts on Some of Life's Higher Issues

By Jeanne de Vietinghoff

Translated by Ethel Ireland Helleman, 1921
Edited and Introduced by Christine Mary McGinley, 2015

Copyright © 2016 by Christine Mary McGinley

Book design by Agent 99 Design

All rights reserved. No part of this book may be reproduced or transmitted in any form or by any means, electronic or mechanical, including photocopying, recording, or by any information storage and retrieval system, without permission in writing from the publisher.

ISBN: 978-0-9972204-0-7

Library of Congress Control Number: 2015957853

Published by Gleam of Light Press, LLC
GleamOfLightPress.com

Printed in the United States of America

Jeanne de Vietinghoff
1875–1926

Photo courtesy of the Egon von Vietinghoff Foundation
(Egon von Vietinghoff, 1903-1994,
"Transcendentalist" painter, son of Jeanne de Vietinghoff)
www.vietinghoff.org

Contents

Introduction i
Preface 3
Good 5
Transgression 31
Circumstances 41
The Action of Man 53
The Miracle of God 59
Barren Days 65
To the Vanquished 69
The Courage to Doubt 75
Hope 79
Our Disappointments 91
Fraud 103
Exceptions 113
The Patience that Endures 117
The Respect for Love 127
Grace and Inspiration 145
Detachment 147
The Quiet Force 153
Certainty 159

Introduction

"There are souls who make us believe the soul exists." These are the words of Marguerite Yourcenar that prompted me to search for anything I could find by the author she spoke of with such admiration in her essay entitled: "In Memory of Diotima: Jeanne de Vietinghoff."

It was also Marguerite Yourcenar who said that sometimes a book can lie dormant for many years in a forgotten corner of a library only to be opened by a person who feels it was written just for them. This was the way I felt about discovering one of the last remaining copies of the only Jeanne de Vietinghoff book in English translation: *The Understanding of Good: Thoughts on Some of Life's Higher Issues* (The John Lane Company, 1921.)

At the time I came upon this obscure book I was immersed in a treasure hunt for words of wisdom that happened to have been written

The Understanding of Good

by women. I was creating a literary mosaic, a dramatic monologue, which would represent the female voice in literature and in life. Jeanne de Vietinghoff's voice became a major part of *The Words of a Woman* (Crown Publishers, 1999.) It is also the part of the book that readers have found most compelling. Virtually every person who has spoken to me about *The Words of a Woman* has wanted to know how they could get their hands on a copy of Jeanne de Vietinghoff's *The Understanding of Good*.

The Understanding of Good, first published in French (*L'Intelligence du Bien*, 2nd edition, 1915) a century ago this year, is indeed written in the language of another time. It has also lost some of its original nuance and meaning that could not quite be captured in English. What's more, it is a work that would require careful reading in any language, in any time. So what is it about this particular book that warrants making it available again after a hundred years of collecting dust? This will be discovered only by readers willing to give to this extraordinary work the time it deserves.

This was the way I first approached *The Understanding of Good*. I continued on, even

Introduction

through difficult passages, hoping to find whatever jewels of wisdom I might uncover. How could I not? The supreme Yourcenar had compared its author to Diotima, the woman who "undertook to explain God to the banqueters of Plato's *Symposium*." As it turned out, I had unearthed much more than a long neglected treasure of a book. Jeanne de Vietinghoff has since remained one of the handful of authors to whom I return whenever I am in need of inspiration.

    Jeanne Bricou was born into an upper class family in Brussels in 1875. Though Protestant, she was educated in a convent school where she showed signs of brilliance at an early age. In her mid-twenties she married the German-Baltic Baron, Conrad von Vietinghoff, and began a life which included giving birth to and rearing two sons, travel throughout Europe, and a continued intense, intellectual life. Though she lived a life of privilege, it was her inner life that consumed all of her energies. Her hunger for spiritual enrichment was so urgent, so impassioned, she could only devote her life to it and surround herself with people who did the same. Her home — over the years in Paris, Wiesbaden, Geneva

The Understanding of Good

and Zurich — was the frequent meeting place of like-minded seekers and the scene of much contemplation of the deeper questions of life.

During her short life (she died of cancer at age fifty) Jeanne de Vietinghoff produced six books: *Impressions d'Ame* (Impressions of a Soul), 1909; *La Liberte Interieure* (Inner Freedom), 1912; *L'Intelligence du Bien* (The Understanding of Good), 1915; *Au Seuil d'un Monde Nouveau* (On the Threshold of a New World), 1923; *L'Autre Devoir: Histoire d'une Ame* (The Other Duty: History of a Soul) 1924; and *Sur L'Art de Vivre* (On the Art of Living), 1927 (posthumous). Though her works were well-received both by readers and critics during her lifetime, Jeanne de Vietinghoff has been virtually forgotten in her home countries and, except for the glimmer of recognition that came through *The Words of a Woman,* completely unknown in other parts of the world. Hers would not be the first important voice to have been silenced for years only to be revived at some future time when her message is most needed:

> In the midst of our busy days we seem unable to pause that we may listen to

Introduction

the soul and seek the invisible truths … Life tends to shackle us, to stifle in us the real being that we are and which it is our duty to emancipate and expand. Once securely fettered…by family ties, by the obligations of our careers…all individual growth is checked and we become the plaything of circumstance… Thus, humanity, instead of being enriched by the blessings it pursues, constantly grows poorer in force, in hope, and in true happiness.

Jeanne de Vietinghoff was one of those rare souls who are able to speak to us about the life of the soul and remind us that this is our true life, the only life that matters. She urges us to look beyond our worldly existence — our circumstances, our life-course, even our relationships — and see that the only thing that can bring us true happiness is our development as spiritual beings. That development, that unfolding of the soul, she insists, can only happen through the constant search for truth and through the effort we invest in listening to our own souls.

The Understanding of Good

The Understanding of Good will appeal to readers who are hungry for spiritual sustenance and open to finding it in places other than the established forms. It will especially appeal to those whose conception of God cannot be contained within established forms. As Marguerite Yourcenar said, "We can learn from this exceptional woman how to disengage ourselves from the external forms in which we enclose God. The higher we rise, the more we hold sway over our beliefs. Ultimately, Jeanne de Vietinghoff came more and more to belong to that invisible church, without a name or dogmas, in which all sincerities live in communion ... She unceasingly evolved from everyday wisdom to a higher wisdom and...from the loving God of little children to the infinite Deity of the sage."

Jeanne de Vietinghoff was a devout believer — in God, in humankind, in the power that drives the universe unceasingly *forward*. Though she remained a Christian throughout her life and speaks of Jesus with the purest reverence, above all, she was a seeker after truth, a lover of truth. Searching, questioning, doubt — these are the indispensible tools, she tells us, of both the ardent believer and the disciple of truth. These

Introduction

are "the filters that purify our faith, giving it a personal value which it would not otherwise have had." "Doubt is the sign of the purest love," she says, "and he who has never known it will not be able to grasp the highest conceptions of the Divine, that which only a tried faith can reveal to him."

In *The Understanding of Good*, Jeanne de Vietinghoff explains that by "understanding" she means "the wisdom of the soul," for it is only through the soul, she asserts, that we achieve true understanding. The "good" she speaks of is not the good that is defined for us by our religious beliefs or by human laws but by the higher authority that speaks to us through our innermost being.

> The more enlightened our perception becomes, the more instinctively it transfers the problem of responsibility from the realm of our common conscience to that of our profoundly individual sense of justice; it no longer concerns itself with what a man ought to do or say but with what he ought to

The Understanding of Good

be in relation to the intimate and divine ideal that exists within him.

The true good, the good that sustains us, does not depend on our poor, vacillating attempts at obedience, charity and faith, but on our fidelity to the universal progress of the ever-increasing good.

Little is known about the philosophical and literary influences in Jeanne de Vietinghoff's life. Clearly, her reading was both wide and deep. Marguerite Yourcenar saw Plato in her. One also sees Plotinus and other followers of Plato who expanded Plato's ideas about the soul. I especially see Ralph Waldo Emerson, so strikingly in fact, it has seemed to me at times that Jeanne de Vietinghoff was channeling Emerson — his ideas about "soul reliance," about the nature of good, the dynamism of truth, the importance of doubt in developing true faith, the law of compensation at play in all of life. Emerson's unique brand of idealism, his emphasis on the life of the soul, his unyielding faith in the good in the soul of man — these

Introduction

are all given new life and force in Jeanne de Vietinghoff's *The Understanding of Good*.

I was not surprised to learn that among Madame Vietinghoff's friends was literary Nobel laureate Maurice Maeterlinck, a devotee of Emerson, who no doubt raised Emersonian thought in many conversations with her. One also sees in her ideas the Eastern thought, which surely emerged in her discussions with Maeterlinck and with Romain Rolland, another literary Nobel laureate who was among her circle of friends and who, like Maeterlinck, searched deeply into the world's great spiritual traditions.

As I imagine those evening gatherings at her home, rich with conversation among Madame and her friends, I feel certain that one of the questions they pursued was this: Are the ideas of the world's great thinkers absorbed by those who follow them and then expressed in new and creative forms? Or are the great thinkers of every time direct receivers of the same universal truths?

Jeanne de Vietinghoff was both an absorber and a receiver. She was also driven to become a communicator. She found that in order to

The Understanding of Good

live a meaningful life, to devote herself to the progress of her soul, she could only become a creative writer.

Where Jeanne de Vietinghoff surpasses even some of the great mystic-writers, in my view, is in her understanding of the human heart and of the role love plays in our spiritual development. It was on this subject that she most assisted me in making the female voice in *The Words of a Woman* the full, rounded voice of a real woman, a woman who had lived and loved deeply. I was especially moved by her statement: "Love, for so many people, simply a fortuitous circumstance, is for others life itself ... For no ambition, no joy can replace that marvelous unfolding which true love brings to the soul."

What woman would not at some time in her life relate deeply with Madame's assertion that "Man looks for repose and distraction in love, while woman seeks in it the unfolding of her being." And who, in the midst of heartbreak would not be consoled by her thought that "Even the wisest are sometimes deceived and are obliged to pass through the hard school of misplaced love." "The quality of love does not

Introduction

depend on the one who inspires it," she assures us, "but on him who feels it."

Jeanne de Vietinghoff achieved a perspective that enabled her to recognize love as a powerful means of "initiation into the high joy of the wise." The key, she tells us, in love as in life, is to rely on "the quiet force within us," the force that renders us completely independent of our life circumstances "by giving us the power to discern and to separate our higher from our lower self." "For we depend less on what happens in our lives," she asserts, "than on what passes in our souls."

In discovering Jeanne de Vietinghoff's poetic philosophy of the soul, I experienced real life being breathed into the ethereal form of a "Shakespeare's sister" — the original impetus for *The Words of a Woman*, which came from Virginia Woolf. To my surprise, this long-neglected female author, Jeanne de Vietinghoff, also crystallized for me what it means to become a creative writer. In *The Understanding of Good* she speaks to every person who has struggled to find his or her own voice, to "develop the truth that is peculiarly ours."

The Understanding of Good

Man becomes a creator when, after the innumerable stages of adaptation to external influences, he finally grasps what is really his own, what he receives as a personal message.

We can only create original and productive art by giving ourselves for what we are and seeking to be worth much in order that we may give much.

In creative writing, as in all things, she contends, we must learn to trust in our own souls.

Yes, in Jeanne de Vietinghoff's 1915 *The Understanding of Good* one hears loud echoes of the preceding century's New England Transcendentalism. One even recognizes in her expression the uniquely Emersonian style, the almost stream of consciousness, which invites the reader into the *process* of thinking. But the thing that strikes me most about Jeanne de Vietinghoff for which I have only Ralph Waldo Emerson as a basis of comparison is the way they were each perceived by the people who knew them. This is where we find the real power behind all of their shared ideas, behind

Introduction

the singleness of their "courage to entertain high hopes and noble dreams." Rarely do we hear, even of great literary sages, that the strongest impression they made was not in what they wrote but in the people they were, in the exemplary way in which they lived their lives. As Yourcenar expressed it of the woman she knew personally, the woman from whom she received the highest inspiration: "There is something much rarer than competence, talent, or even genius — and that is nobility of soul."

Jeanne de Vietinghoff's *The Understanding of Good* is a work we may return to again and again for the deeper understanding we find each time. It is a work that convinces us not only of the nobility of the soul through which such truths found expression but also of the higher source from which they came.

Christine Mary McGinley
November 6, 2015

"In memory of Diotima: Jeanne de Vietinghoff" is included in Marguerite Yourcenar's *That Mighty Sculptor, Time*, translated by Walter Kaiser. (Farrar, Straus & Giroux, Inc., 1992)

It is with a deep sense of indebtedness to Ethel Ireland Helleman, the 1921 translator of this book, that I have approached the editing of her work for this new edition of Jeanne de Vietinghoff's *The Understanding of Good*. I hope that the minor edits I have made will make this extraordinary piece of literature slightly more readable for today's reader. For those passages for which I have been at a loss for a way to do this without risking misinterpretation, I have left Ms. Helleman's translation untouched. It was her interpretation, after all, that struck me as an enormous gift — as I hope it will you.

The Understanding of Good

Jeanne de Vietinghoff

Preface

Those who may seek in these pages a philosophy or a religion will be inevitably disappointed. It has not been my aim to construct a system or impose a trend; I have only desired to see for myself the truth of the moment and to tell what I have seen in the single wish to serve truth.

I respect the experience of each and all. It is impossible that truth should appear the same to all. Truth is movement; for each an individual movement.

I have called this volume "The Understanding of Good" because without understanding, sincerity and goodwill do not suffice to reveal to us what is right. By understanding I mean that wisdom of the soul — as distinct from that of the mind — which only life experience and communion with the Divine can teach us.

Good

The rich vegetation spread in variegated beauty along the streams, over the plains and up the hillsides, mingling the odors of spring with the hum of insects and the song of birds; and nature, smiling, contented, bathed in light, bloomed under the warm skies. And in the cool shade of this virginal nature the source of good lay in mysterious sleep. Hers was the quickening soul that gave to the forests their perfume and to the wayside flowers their smile.

Man was part of creation; he was happy with the gladness of the flowers and birds, enchanted with all: the vigor of his body, the softness of his mossy bed, the shining of daylight, the green vastness of the plains. He felt himself at one with nature; he accomplished nothing good, he simply rested in the universal good as the child rests in the bosom of a virtuous family whose orders and

The Understanding of Good

habits he accepts without question, convinced that nothing exists outside the small world of which he is part and to which he clings with all the fibers of his being.

But the spirit demands something more than unconscious contentment.

On the day predestined for its evolution, the humble source of good gushed forth, troubling the calm assurance of the complacent world and causing the heart of man to tremble as he became conscious for the first time of the limitless powers of his own mind. It was but as a lightning flash, yet it wiped forever from his brow the tranquility of his happy days. A new power had seized him; and as it grew he was forced to loosen the bonds that bound him to his mother, Nature, and to choose his own path; to fight, to suffer — to be.

From thenceforth the lark sang his morning song in vain. In vain the sun gilded his sanctuary; man heeded neither lark nor sun; doubt had entered his heart, doubt of his primitive past, born of the discovery of a higher state. Did something, then, exist other than he had hitherto known? Strange transition from unconsciousness to consciousness! That

Good

doubt was to call forth a desire; the desire to know that which is greater than himself — and desire forces him to action. He realizes that he is free to act; that he alone, in all nature, has the power to develop or defile the preexistent good. And this action must bring rupture, error: disobedience to established law.

So man had arrived at self-realization, consciousness of the personality that differentiates him from all his surroundings. His ego was in a state of rude primitiveness, the product of natural egoism, which says "I will," but knows not yet what he wills or why he wills it. But the act of volition suffices to cause the breach of law. It is the first step toward disorder, destruction, death; but also toward triumph. "He who has not fully lived can neither fully die nor be reborn."

The awakening of the soul first reveals itself by a desire for truth. Conscious now of his vocation, man wishes to become perfect. His means of realizing this ideal is effort; his guide, law. He must endeavor to understand this law and to fulfill it in its utmost detail. This means a schooling of the will to which every force must be bent, in order to overcome the

The Understanding of Good

so-called dangerous instincts and develop the lawful virtues.

Having once achieved this formidable task, man has succeeded in making of his life a finished example. But what strange mystery is here! His heart is no longer satisfied, for under the spurious weight of a forced activity all that was natural and instinctive in him has withered and come to naught.

The struggle to obey has increased his force, but the disillusion which his experience of arbitrary good brings has turned him from the accepted standards of virtue. Bruised, deceived, he is no longer willing to follow an illusory law; he must be himself and seek his own truth. A perilous adventure on which he may stray far, suffer hard knocks, and inevitably draw down on himself the world's disapproval.

The spirit demands more than established order. Infringement of the law is a necessity, it is a logical result of the affirmation of personal life; it is often an error and always painful.

The first assertion of personality which forces us to think and to be ourselves is nearly always looked on as a fault, because it runs counter to existing order. But nevertheless it is

Good

a necessary fault without which progress would be impossible. There are virtues that can only be born from error; riches that are only to be gained by temporary loss. Infringement of the law is at once the result and the condition of the birth of the soul. Truly, every new idea is a violation of some older idea, as the awakening of tomorrow is a violation of today's slumber. As long as man continues to evolve, in other words, to separate himself from chaos, to express himself in a higher form, he must always shatter something. In shattering, he disobeys; in breaking, he creates.

"For it must be that offences come," Jesus said. Without evil man would have remained in a state of vegetation. "But woe to him through whom they come!" Suffering is the inevitable consequence.

In rare and pure natures like that of Jesus the emancipation of personal thought justifies itself by the force of the soul that has produced it: the natural transition from a primitive to a higher state. And though His soul may have been without error, men did not always think so. Doubtless there were many who reproached the child Jesus for His forgetfulness of Mary

The Understanding of Good

and Joseph when He tarried in the temple, "busy with His Father's affairs."

Natural egoism, in its supreme indifference, breaks the law for the sake of its own enjoyment; hallowed egoism breaks it through necessity and is prepared to wound, if need be, in order to create the higher life for which it is destined.

Pure or impure, the soul must accept its Calvary. In the moment when it foresees its final goal it accepts the responsibility and the horror of the consequences of its own volition, and acknowledges even its own condemnation.

We do not always know why we act; sometimes a secret instinct will even give us distinct warning of the suffering our actions will bring upon us. Yet we act, and with entire conviction, because an irresistible force urges us, in spite of ourselves, toward the accomplishment of our supreme destiny.

The revolt which is forced on us by the voice of progress may present itself to us under different forms: infraction of the social conventions, emancipation from parental authority, or challenge of the current morality; different for each, these rebellions are necessary

Good

for all, just as new growth is threatened by the acceptance of existing standards.

The existence of evil in the world is undoubtedly necessary for the unfolding of good. It is better that the individual should openly display his imperfections in the form of mistakes than that he should disguise them; conventional and artificial control has never produced more than the semblance of virtue.

A fault that stirs us is better than a virtue that sends us to sleep.

It is in fact impossible to advance without erring; a child too strictly guarded can hardly develop; a man who withdraws from contact with life on the grounds of religious or social duties can never have more than a borrowed virtue: he may understand the theory of virtue, but he is ignorant of its practice. His faultless life is the expression of a soul without value.

When the sculptor chisels his marble in order to release the form his inspiration has taken, he scatters around him a thousand broken fragments. The faults of our conscious life, amongst which our spiritual being expands, resemble this accumulation of splinters round a masterpiece.

The Understanding of Good

To be occupied solely with the outward correctness of one's life is to resemble the sculptor who fears to put the tool on the marble lest he should disarrange his studio.

In the spiritual, as in the material realm, one must dare in order to succeed: dare to see, to believe, to doubt, to love, to suffer and to be. "The kingdom of heaven is to the strong." We must dare, even at the risk of falling into error — dare and be ready to admit our errors and atone for them.

The champion of our outward order becomes the enemy of individual good as soon as he attacks sincerity. A fault is not always a fall; indeed, when it is committed by a sincere soul seeking truth, it is more often a stepping-stone to higher ground. It only becomes harmful to the progress of the soul when it lessens the intensity of life and defiles the purity of our aspirations. Is such failure possible to the really noble soul? Will not its worth, garnered surely through many lives of struggle, rise beyond passing error? Does the instrument lose its value because a clumsy hand brings discord from it? Must the soul inevitably deteriorate when the conscience deviates? We

Good

can only lose that which is not truly a part of us; many a virtue, for instance, those on which we most pride ourselves. Can a man return to childhood? Those who have once made truth their own can never be false to it without forsaking themselves. The virtue that is once truly ours is beyond our power; it is part of us.

"Let the tares grow with the good grain." Good and bad, the seeds must germinate and grow together so that we may be able to distinguish and separate them. Leaning toward evil, yearning for good; the secret of victory lies in the increase of our vital power.

Infringement of the law is always painful. Man was the cause of evil; he is also its victim; one day he will be its conqueror.

Our fidelity to the impulses of the new life will bring suffering: it exposes us to blunders by bringing us face to face with countless possibilities while we are still inexperienced; it leads us into isolation because every appeal to life will be judged as a revolt against moral and religious routine. Above all, it demands continual sacrifice.

Truth can never be cheaply bought. As soon as the soul seeks to substantiate its true

The Understanding of Good

essence, it must be prepared to accept defeat and privation. But in the teeth of this defeat the spiritual man breaks his bonds and forces a passage toward a larger future, a fuller destiny.

The birth of the spirit, which constrains us to emerge from the torpor of matter and enter the arena where souls struggle to unfold, is one of the greatest trials we can be called upon to endure.

Our primitive nature contents itself with tangible benefits, but no sooner has the spirit unveiled the world of invisible blessings than our desires begin to soar; yet the higher they mount, the more difficult they are to satisfy.

The disproportion existing between our increasing aspirations and our limited resources demands constant sacrifice from us and finally destroys in us the lower self: egoism.

The soul, awakening, finds itself faced with three possibilities: the resignation of its ideal, thereby accepting the current mediocrity; the creation of an illusory ideal by refusing to see things as they are; or, to risk being crushed by remaining faithful to itself and appraising mankind at its true value. Only a really pure soul seems capable of confronting this cruel

Good

contradiction; and this, not from inclination or a sense of duty, but because it is constrained by its very nature to prefer death to the loss of its ideal.

The deadly shock arising from the encounter of the highest conceptions with brutal realities is the supreme injustice, for it is the chastisement of good. But it is only at the price of this long death of starvation that the spirit can triumph, even as the flower can only unfold through the withering of its sheath.

In the material world it is possible to enjoy ill-gotten gains; in the invisible world there are no unearned fortunes. There we live by our labor, we become rich by our sacrifice; the soul gathers light, force and glory in proportion to the depth to which sorrow has delved therein. This sorrow is of great avail.

"The pure in heart shall see God," and, God inspiring their thoughts, they no longer need to question man or to fulfill his laws. They live the truth, they *are* the Good.

The heart is purified according to its sincerity. Through suffering it casts off all it holds of distress, falsehood, sophistry; for suffering, voluntarily accepted, frees the heart

The Understanding of Good

from all imperfections, leaving it only its original aspirations.

It is not the descent into the depths of anguish but the courage to remain in that cruel abyss that confers on the soul its true value. This sorrow is not everlasting.

We have accustomed ourselves to connect our idea of happiness with outward advantages rather than with inner realities, and we are inclined to doubt the justice of that fate which holds spiritual beauty as its only reward.

Yet it does not follow that because the spiritual birth brings us invisible benefits it therefore deprives us of the prizes of this world. The sacrifice claimed by the soul is not final; it marks the passage from a lower to a higher state, in which our transformed faculties enable us to see everything with new eyes.

Man is born matter; he must struggle in order to become spirit: when the man's spirit is mature, he restores Nature's rights and becomes master of all things, for he has conquered evil, the cause of all his prohibitions. Thenceforth he may enjoy as his due, all the benefits he has hitherto unjustly seized; for he no longer claims them by weakness or

Good

ignorance but in the deliberate fullness of his strength. He is no longer a child who obeys but a master who commands.

In natural man the life of the soul is smothered by the life of the body; the man whose will is developed may often find his natural life forced into the background. This conflict underlies all suffering. But in the harmonious life of the future, body and soul will be one, for that which separated them, evil, will have been overcome.

Conflict having ceased, the regenerated man is at once body and soul; the body is no longer an offense to the soul, nor the soul antagonistic to the body; for the body has accepted immolation from the soul, and the soul, triumphant, has raised up the tortured body. Man, now having come into his spiritual rights, is authorized to assume temporal rights.

The soul says to the body: "Since thou hast renounced all, thou shalt possess all; through death thou hast won the dignity of life; I could not do otherwise than destroy those selfish instincts that had never known sorrow; today, purified by sacrifice, thou shalt know the fulfillment of thy legitimate desires; thou didst

The Understanding of Good

thwart my triumph, therefore I laid chains on thee, burdened thee with sickness, exposed thee to inexorable laws, robbing thee of all joy; now that thou hast learnt submission, see, I break thy fetters and make thee to share my glory; for I need thee, as thou needest me. Together we will create the perfect harmony of the material and spiritual spheres and remake the earthly paradise."

The presence of good, quiescent in Nature, is the state of primitive happiness; the development of good brings rupture with Nature, hence, suffering; the fruition of good is the return to Nature, but to a Nature infinitely exalted; it is perfect harmony.

This harmony is produced without our knowledge by the growth of that good which germinates in us; and one day we find ourselves possessed of all we had vainly sought to acquire by our obedience to external law.

And henceforth our whole striving will be toward this soul-expansion; our efforts will be concentrated on the restoration in us of the childlike life, to the purging from it of all false expression, and to providing it with the freedom essential for its growth and fruition. And

Good

here it is our duty to sacrifice and overthrow everything that is an obstacle to the unfolding of the new life, even the most legitimate aspiration or the purest law. The inner call is urgent, impassioned; and on our obedience to it hangs our eternal life.

Good is not a finished product but a continually expanding power. At all times its progressive stages have been heralded by pioneers who, leaving the trodden paths, have groped their way alone toward the glimmering of the new light. And so humanity takes a step onward.

In the same way, good in the heart of man can only advance with a slow and almost imperceptible motion. Our intellect may conceive an ideal, our will may strive after it, but to live it we must wait patiently till our soul shall have acquired the force, the greatness and the purity necessary for its realization. Whenever we seek to precipitate its evolution by accepting ready-made truth, or practicing a virtue that is beyond our power, we must inevitably deteriorate.

Something we too often forget, especially in our relations with our fellow creatures, is to

The Understanding of Good

recognize the stage of the other's development and afford them the patience due to the progress of good. Let us ask from each other only simple honesty in the phase we are each passing through, and no more.

Though nobody can give us truth, it sometimes happens that, when we have actually lived certain truths, we find their confirmation in the experience of others; and this corroboration validates them in our own mind.

The child, who in the beginning shared in the parental gains, having become adult, must in its turn earn its own livelihood; and in the same way, man, roused by the call of good and matured by suffering, must work to discriminate, choose and win for himself a personal and vital share of the universal truth.

He can only gain this experience by measuring his own power with the world-forces. The educative contact of life will develop his unconscious qualities; they will become an integral part of him, as his limbs are one with his body. Lawful owner of his share of personal good, earned through experience, he is immune from external influence and is thenceforth capable of accomplishing his true destiny.

Good

All good is the birth and development of divine life in us; the discovery, by faith, of the spiritual world. Primitive man clings to outward appearances. To him, motion means life, to smile means to be happy, a good action is synonymous with good. But in the exercise of our physical powers a new ego awakes in us, a new world opens before our eyes, and we know that a silence, a tear, an obstacle, may mean a greater joy.

Matter, having become transparent, allows us to distinguish the soul of things, and we feel that soul vibrate in unison with our own, like the echo of a single voice reverberating from end to end of the immortal spheres. This progressive initiation into the unseen realities constitutes true progress, and our conquests in these marvelous lands form our true realm.

If it were not for the falseness of appearances and the weight of our encumbered reason, our natural intuition, establishing contact between the universal divinity and the divine in us, would lead us in triumph to flawless beauty. But as members of the human race we must reckon with obstacles; and, as parts of an organism, our higher being must suit its flight

The Understanding of Good

to the step of our lower self. It may be that our transcendental self, having scarcely got beyond its infancy, still needs the control of human logic and the shackles of daily life to hold it back from vain wanderings.

Nevertheless, the secret instinct, named in turned, "intuition," "inspiration," "grace," by morality, art and religion, remains the greatest, the most real and possibly the only immortal part of us. It is the instrument of progress and the truth of the future — that truth which must prevail against all the conquests of force, reason and intelligence.

He will have lived for good who in spite of a thousand hindrances shall have given his soul the greatest chances of awakening; and he for evil who in spite of an apparently blameless life has hindered the unfolding of the divine within himself.

Nature is a divine work; we are born with the germ of good in us. The good we do on earth is therefore an unfolding of our true nature, an expansion of our highest and most essential self. It is not a duty but a joy; a joy, certainly, won painfully in a world where all is thwarted,

Good

but a joy that enlightened man should seek as naturally as he seeks happiness.

Our innermost being, dedicated to good, can find its permanent satisfaction nowhere else.

And yet this being, so pure, gardener of a sacred seed, is one with the defiled world that endeavors to destroy it by holding up false ideals. And just as the growth of the true in Nature has brought forth the good, so has the perversion of natural desires produced the evil, the reign of fraud that underlies all our griefs.

The mysterious presence of fundamentally evil beings amongst us is explained by the waste material left by Nature in her forward march: ashes fallen where the fierce flame has passed, empty chrysalises where the butterfly has flown, offscourings of the errors that accompany all progress.

The duty of man is to discover the germ of primitive truth amidst the universal falsehood, and to extricate it, like a nugget of gold, in order that it may be given the setting and the glory of a royal gem.

When he has regained his early and true aspirations, man will find his essential self again, and with it, the Good. Thus, every striving

The Understanding of Good

after happiness, however distorted it may be, is fundamentally only a reaching out towards the Good, a yearning for the lost paradise.

The good is always the object of your desires; but like a little child you can mistake the hyssop for the honey; hence it has been necessary to express truth by laws and laws by words; but he to whom all words are familiar may find himself as far from great thoughts as one who, obeying the law, may yet find himself far from the understanding of the Good.

Man's great danger lies in knowledge and in his liberty to use it as he will. Knowledge may estrange him from good, but it may equally lead him to it, provided he remains humble and conscious of his own fallibility.

What most alienates us from truth is to use knowledge with self-interest as our motive. Disinterestedness is the first condition of all good. I must learn to desire, not from love of pleasure but from love of beauty, and then I shall discover that beauty is itself the most perfect of all pleasures.

Most of us agree to attribute to evil all the powers and to good all the weaknesses; it is the old story of the wolf and the lamb. And since

Good

we have assisted with the oppression of the just for centuries, no one shows much surprise at the apparent failure of good; and if it ventures to claim its right to supremacy it is at once regarded with suspicion.

It is admitted that good includes all of the passive qualities: gentleness, humility, unselfishness, patience; it is a combination of inoffensive virtues, free to propagate, like the flowers in a garden, for the enjoyment of all. But do we remember that in its essence it is a force, a will, a power destined to triumph through strife?

Nowadays the virtuous man is apt to be a somewhat anemic creature; he has lost faith in himself, no longer sure of the purpose assigned to him. He fears to show himself as he is and humbly begs from clowns the permission to pass. He only dares to assert himself when sustained by the Church or protected by the law. He wastes the strength of his heroism in petty virtues and exhausts the consciousness of his royal mission in unhealthy emotion.

The evil-doer, more courageous and independent, forces his way in the teeth of opposition, and so surmounts the obstacles

The Understanding of Good

of established order. This man knows what he wants and spares no means to gain his end. The followers of virtue might well follow his example in imitating his audacity, for goodwill without strength often does more harm than actual evil.

The conception of good consists for most people in the official dictates of the current morality; it is not a truth lived, individual, different from the common experience. And yet strength does not come to us from our adherence to the common good, but from the energy we give to developing the truth that is peculiarly ours. For though good is adaptable to the generality of men, in order to become effectual it must be tested, one might almost say, recreated, by each personality.

Just as good cannot remain a vague and general entity, it is not satisfied with a false brotherly love. It is not by coddling the feeble and deploring human misery that we become truly useful to our fellow creatures, but by having faith in and asserting justice.

A perennial law decrees that every growing thing must crush what remains small around it: the forest tree, spreading its mighty branches,

Good

smothers many a frail bush; and genius, in the pursuit of its ideal, treads down the vulgar interests lying in its path; and the enlightened conscience, asserting itself, shocks and wounds the ignorant. Such force often appears cruel, but it is vindicated by the fact that it aids the true progress of humanity.

This is the force, capable of great feats, of bearing all responsibilities in perfect independence, which is still lacking in the conception of good.

The more profound and subtle an idea is, the more easily it can give rise to error: there is perhaps no conception which, in passing through the narrow filter of our brain, has been so mutilated and cramped as the conception of good.

Our conscience has perhaps somewhat outgrown that of the barbarian, who, after strangling his brother, offers up prayers for his mania and passes on contentedly; but it has not yet conceived good except in the ephemeral and variable form of human law, and believes its duty done when it has taken stock of its little store of current morality.

The Understanding of Good

Good does not lie in the accomplishment of a circumscribed law, but in the acceptance of the increasing and universal life; it is the development of the eternal germ in us, the birth of a life whose authority so surpasses the old order that it absolves us from the current conceptions of good and evil and gives us a new understanding of all values.

Evil does not consist in the infringement of the law but in the denial of life, in all that hinders its development and its exaltation: in cold reason that kills ardor, in materialism that deadens, indolence that paralyzes, egoism that seizes, and falsehood that distorts.

In order to understand the power and the value of good, we must root out the idea of its visible and tangible manifestation. The true good, the good that sustains us, does not depend on our poor, vacillating attempts at obedience, charity and faith, but on our fidelity to the universal progress of the ever-increasing good. As life is in the plant, so is good in us, and it will speed us, when we have once surrendered ourselves to its power, through all the joyous or disturbing fluctuations of existence, toward the fulfillment of our supreme destiny.

Good

Good is the mighty stream of life: emerging from the hidden depths of the universe, it pours its fructifying flood over the earth, to plunge at last into the infinite ocean of eternity, forever one with God.

Transgression

There are two kinds of wrongdoing: the one offends against our soul, the other injures our external life. The sin against the soul is a treason toward our intimate, profound ideal, altering our real value for years, possibly even existences; the sin against life is caused by a temporary deviation of conscience, which need not necessarily lower our soul but which always leads to suffering and the penalty attached to all blunders. A child plays with fire and is burnt; he suffers because he has disobeyed; but that disobedience, far from undermining his moral development, often aids, as it forces him to realize the character and meaning of the things around him.

And no doubt the fact that sins against life do not always involve treason to the soul explains why they are seldom followed by remorse, especially in a strong character that knows its own worth. So we will not attribute

The Understanding of Good

too great an importance to this form of transgression. We can leave to social justice the duty of repressing what is held to be harmful. But when we sit in judgment on the conduct of our brother, let us do our best to keep in mind only the motives that have produced it. Doubtless we have all seen great faults committed by very excellent people without any change in their fundamental value having taken place: erring, they have been their own judges and have not lowered their ideal to the level of their action. On the other hand, how often all the virtues are vainly practiced by the mediocre!

These facts prove to us that the touchstone is not to be found where we look for it and that there is a world of difference between visible error and real sin. Where is the dividing line between the superficial transgression which is born and dies within a life, and a spiritual sin whose consequences the soul bears beyond the limits of our conception? We know not, for this boundary varies according to the stuff of which the individual is made. And so our verdict will never be just. But what we can with such difficulty decide for others we feel with absolute clarity when it concerns ourselves; we

Transgression

know why our conscience is merciless at certain moments toward a failing or transgression, while at other times it is ready to pass by a crime unobserved, even though the crime may have caused great unhappiness to another.

The more enlightened our perception becomes, the more instinctively it transfers the problem of responsibility from the realm of our common conscience to that of our profoundly individual sense of justice; it no longer concerns itself with what a man ought to do or say but with what he ought to be in relation to the intimate and divine ideal that exists within him.

Real transgression is an unseen, profound and infinitely subtle act that happens in the secret place of our being; it is a falsehood of the soul, a wrong we do, not to others, but to ourselves. We are guilty of it every time we disobey what we have recognized as being the best and highest in us; our thoughts, words and acts thenceforth are simply the expression of that moment of infidelity.

We cannot sin outside our soul, and those who see us steal or betray will never know the hour and the manner of our real transgression.

The Understanding of Good

This inner lie is more frequently caused by the lack of will to do well than by any actual desire to do evil. Those who desire evil are rare; men generally seek only their own self-interest, their advantage, their happiness; but — and here begins the transgression — they desire these things at any price, even the price of honor: they desire in egoism.

As one can lie to God in the mere inaction of one's soul, so one can injure one's fellow creatures without words and without deeds. This transgression has nothing to do with external life which, indeed, often seems to flourish most when the richest flowers of the inner garden are dying.

Many people have claimed to see, in this unjust contradiction between the course of external life and the movements of the soul, the intervention of a malign power, bent on favoring the least scrupulous. Is it not rather a logical sequence of cause and effect? He who longs for riches sees his affairs prosper through the fact that he gives more energy to them; and the soul, anxious for progress, unconsciously chooses the circumstances most

Transgression

favorable to its development, even at the expense of worldly happiness.

But if our inner loyalty has no direct action on our destiny, it is nevertheless, for him who guards it, a source of abundance and a means of reaching a higher happiness. Often a noble aspiration, such as a disinterested love or a sacrifice, has sufficed to maintain the soul's balance through all its errors. Yet nothing is more susceptible than a noble feeling. And a harsh gesture, trivial enough to all appearance, suffices to lower our moral level. Its repetition ends by undermining virtue's most beautiful edifice.

Do you remember an evening of long ago, when, gazing earnestly into the eyes of the well-beloved, you beheld the beauty and comprehended the worth of life? All that was mediocre vanished; the earth was a new place where, with buoyant step, you scaled the luminous summits; then weariness fell on you, the vision was obscured. Pressed by a thousand outside claims, your eyes closed to the brilliance of the firmament. Sorrowfully, perchance, but resolutely, you turned away from the ideal you

The Understanding of Good

had glimpsed to follow the common path of paltry interests and prudent ambitions.

A moment only had the vision held you, but in spurning it you decided your destiny. Fate! say you; ignorance, per chance! And from that moment you changed and your aspirations changed with you; more robust and less sensitive, with increased activity and diminished susceptibility, you became more satisfied but less happy. And your life's course was turned aside. Hostile to your soaring dreams, fortune now smiled on your moderate desires.

It may be that you felt ill at ease in that state of natural prosperity; the unselfish ideal, even if only once seen, leaves forever a certain longing deep down in the heart. Perhaps you have fallen into many errors, but the real transgression is that of which you were guilty on that forgotten evening when for the first time you betrayed the truth within the secret sanctuary of your soul.

I seek to recognize my brother and I no longer find in his glance the depth of far-off dreams or the weariness of noble struggles. His firm step, his hardened features no longer betray the spirit. Is my brother dead or does he

Transgression

only slumber in a deep dungeon where captive souls await the visit of a new savior? How much was his choice free and how much forced on him? For the fetters that bind us within are also around us, and to break them we need the help of a force not bestowed on us in equal measure. And if a man has really denied God, how far has he realized and regretted his faithlessness? Do the disorders of the spirit and the errors of conscience actually harm the soul, or do they only delay it in doubt and sadness on the pathway of salvation? Who shall say?

All that passes in the core of our being is so subtle and elusive, we can hardly know and far less judge the cause, the origin and progress of evil in a soul. Who knows whether those souls we call lost have not vainly sought to tell us what oppressed them, and have at last felt forced to resign themselves to failure because they have not been able to call for help?

Not by measuring our knowledge but by admitting the grandeur of the unknowable and telling ourselves that we depend entirely on it shall we attain the full amplitude of our soul and the greatest measure of justice in our life.

The Understanding of Good

Let us then pay heed, not to our actions or words or thoughts, but to the faint shadows that pass secretly across the threshold of the Holy of holies. As soon as our sense of beauty is dimmed, or languor paralyzes our triumphant enthusiasm; as soon as we become less good, less loving, less pure, less generous in our impulses, less sincere and whole in our giving, we may be sure that danger is nigh. Let us halt, and listen to the heart of our childhood. That alone is always true!

It is not always by his life or even by the development of his soul that we can estimate the value of a human creature; in order to be just, we should be able to compare the results he has obtained with the chances that were afforded him. The merit of a man lies in his love of good, whatever form or manifestation it may take. There are those for whom the fulfilling of the law is a joy, a necessity; to others it is a stern effort; and again there are some to whom it is an error. And all this depends upon a mysterious combination of circumstances, habits, influences — of spiritual experiences which have built up in them the idea of good. That "conception of good," possessed by all of

Transgression

us under different guises, is in a manner the divine seal for which we ought all to learn a mutual respect; for though the form of truth adopted by our brothers may be open to criticism, the experience they have lived by their truth remains forever sacred.

He who longs after truth, even if he deceives himself, seeks the light; but he who deliberately commits evil shuts his soul to all that could enlighten it, for he counts on darkness to conceal the consequences of his faults; and where is a more favorable shade or a more discreet silence to be found than in those regions of the inward conscience where none can penetrate? But however pleasing our dwelling may be, we can find no joy there if the warmth and light necessary to happiness are banished from it. We have the power to spread a veil between ourselves and the world, but not between our soul and our self. And does not our happiness depend much more on our own soul than on the souls of others?

Evil in the sphere of morals is all that is false and artificial, that seeks to conceal what it really is, to appear what it is not. It is all that

The Understanding of Good

is not simple, natural and human, all that lies, whether with good or evil intent.

Circumstances

Life tends to shackle us, to stifle in us, perhaps by family ties, by the obligations of our career, or by social and religious influences, the real being that we are, and which it is our duty to emancipate and expand. Once securely fettered we are lost; all individual growth is checked and we become the plaything of circumstances. Sometimes these circumstances can be modified, but more often they are irremediable; yet we always have the power to dominate them. In the midst of this chaos, how can we achieve a possibility of existence for our veritable self?

When we have tried every means of escape from the prison in which fate has chained us, nothing but resignation remains. But by casting off our chains, in other words, by living our inner life as if we were free creatures, our soul does break free. For the soul has the marvelous privilege of being able to reject circumstances

The Understanding of Good

and to create for itself a paradise, even in the midst of the most arid desert. Sometimes, even, the force emanating from the soul ends by influencing events, and thus creates a new atmosphere, a second destiny.

For we have two destinies, as we have two natures: one that has its origin in our primitive self and is with us even in the cradle — a lingering reflection of a former existence — and the other, higher destiny which radiates from our developed personality. The first hinders our true aspirations while the other, on the contrary, responds to and aids them.

The feeble souls who have not been able either to free themselves or achieve creative power, often remain crushed beneath the weight of a primitive and arbitrary nature; they perceive a thousand possibilities of deliverance, but their impotent dreams cannot materialize on the physical plane and so are powerless to change their surroundings. Strong souls know how to create a domain independent of matter. Who has not sometime experienced the strange sensation of escaping from outside happenings and of living, as it were, outside his own life? If we are sometimes able to bear a situation that is

Circumstances

humanly untenable, it is because *we* — our *real self* — is untouched by it. It is that real self, that infinitely small, infinitely true something in us which will rule the future and impose its mark upon our destiny.

At first there is a fierce struggle, a stubborn fury of the forces of the past against our growing individuality; but gradually they become dulled and we find ourselves less sensitive to old influences, with which are already merged elements of another kind: friendship, occupations, circumstances appear in another light. It is as though we enter a new era where fate has other habits, another manner. One feels a stranger in one's own life; till, suddenly, a sense of familiarity with the scene awakens a remembrance of the far-off dream. Has God given substance to our supreme thought?

As we advance, the way becomes clearer and we experience one of those sudden changes of fortune that astound the onlooker no less than ourselves. It is almost as if Fate, understanding at last with whom she has to deal, seeks to adapt events to our veritable needs.

The Understanding of Good

Yet in order to realize his dream, even the strongest soul must wait till life has paid its debt to the past. It is thus that we often sow without reaping and reap where we have not sown; "we reap as we have sown" possibly in a former life, and sow what we shall only reap in a life still to come. So even if our fate cannot yet follow our soul, sooner or later it will rejoin it and, either in this life or in another, we shall finally live that which we are.

We must all bow to the inevitable, but the will that survives defeat has an infinitely greater power than the will that triumphs; and the just man who accepts defeat rises above circumstances and imposes his spirit on the very obstacle that has bruised him.

Much patience is needed to await the shaping of things around us to the form of our thoughts; but if those thoughts are sincere, all that is inferior to them must end by submitting to them. The power of unconscious merit is after all the only power that can be exerted between man and man. It is not uncommon to hear even sorely tried people say that they have obtained all they desired from life. It is the character

Circumstances

of the picture that decides its frame; only a mediocre canvas will have an indifferent frame.

Let us give up, if need be, the removal of the hindrances, but never the conquering of them — the advance in spite of them! Someone has said: "We must submit to nothing but happiness."

Fate, though often obeying us, will not allow us to do her any violence; the attacks we make on her in a moment of impatience or revolt or discouragement, are sure to fail and will recoil on us. Let us not treat her as an enemy, but as an ally. Let us seek to understand her, to enter into her intentions, not that we may do violence to them, but use them. If she closes the highway that would lead us straight to our goal, perhaps a roundabout way will also lead us there; the key is not to wait in fear and trembling at closed doors. The hindrances we meet with are not meant to break us but to make us flexible, to teach us to adapt ourselves to everything while remaining our true selves. For one thing is denied to us only that we may discover another. Fate is against the stubborn, the ignorant and the feeble; she has little power over the wise man, for he no longer

The Understanding of Good

depends on her; his treasure is elsewhere. His real life is within.

Obstacles are not the only things that bar the road to happiness; our efforts must often be directed within and not without, against the feelings that oppress us. The chain that we cannot break by exterior force is often destined to be loosened inwardly. There are blessings which we ought never to give up but which we must learn at times to do without while still continuing to hope and to live.

It is not always in our power to instantly suppress either external obstacles or inner hindrances, even when we see them clearly. All progress is the result of long effort. Much time is needed for the acquisition of the intelligence and the power demanded by a higher state. And this is the trial in which faith is often shipwrecked.

It is possible to consider a circumstance from several points of view. Our understanding of it depends on the measure of acceptance we bring to it; and this depends on our conception of the true purpose of things. If we have grasped the fact that a disagreeable circumstance can be filled with meaning, we

Circumstances

accept it and allow our soul to receive the lessons it brings. To understand is to forgive, to accept, to expand inwardly; to understand is to order the course of our inner life according to the progress of the vast wheel of destiny, without resistance or struggle. It is to be at one with God, to recognize his wisdom as greater than ours.

Let us have confidence in nature and allow the good that slumbers in us to come to life. Some seeds, falling into the crevice of a rock, without soil, air or light, crushed under stones, still manage to grow and to blossom. And do we have less power for good than the humble seed? Are the obstacles to our development more unyielding than stones?

We give too much power to external actions and circumstances, and our restlessness with life is a hindrance to divine action. In the midst of our busy days we seem unable to pause that we may listen to the soul and seek the invisible truths. Thus, humanity, instead of being enriched by the blessings it pursues, constantly grows poorer in force, in hope and in true happiness.

The Understanding of Good

Useful as it is for us to learn to work in order to earn our daily bread, it is just as necessary that we be ready to cease working so that we may gain the bread of life. Just as the labor of man produces his body's sustenance, so do the hours of inaction, of silence and contemplation alone teach him to keep his equilibrium and achieve his happiness.

The great challenge of life, after that of knowing oneself, is to find a suitable environment for one's soul. Without this effort, many of our faculties can never expand.

Circumstances, contrary or favorable, have not the right to threaten our life; let us then not give them more importance than they deserve.

Circumstances are the garments of life; they change their form and color, are torn and become worn out. But true happiness pursues its way as the heart of man beats beneath whatever vesture of joy or sorrow he may wear.

Events have no real power over our soul. Rather, it is within our power to regulate their action on our soul according to our reception of them and to make of them our allies or our enemies.

Circumstances

We imagine our grief to be irremediable, for instance, because we ignore the manifold sources of joy still springing in the heart that seems dead and in the world that seems so empty.

To be discouraged in the face of a circumstance, however adverse, is to prove the narrowness of our horizon and the shortness of our vision. It is not circumstances in themselves that so oppress us but the rigid expectations by which we surround them. It appears to us as if sickness must exclude all joy of life, that disappointment poisons the springs of the heart irrevocably, that the loss of our fortune entails eternal poverty on us — as if that joy, that affection and that abundance had not their real source far more in ourselves than in any outward concerns.

I possess all, wherever I may be, if I am able to feel all; for we depend less on what happens in our life than on what passes in our soul.

If I am able to control the idea we commonly hold of things, can I not by the same power control the things themselves? We should free ourselves not only from the ideas of others but also from our own; for there is a

The Understanding of Good

great gulf between the genuine ideas suggested by our own soul and the parasitic notions with which our environment is saturated.

It is not the task of circumstances to crush us but to teach us to control them. Let us sharpen our spirit and fortify our will so that we may forge a passage through their opposing flood.

If the will is strong enough to endure, it will end by justifying itself and attaining its purpose. If I desire life (and I can never escape this duty) the death around me will be obliged to withdraw. And if my gaze summons the light, dawn will not tarry to emerge from night.

Perhaps discouragement is only the ignorance of the half-unhappy who know not how to rise from the abyss because they have never reached the bottom of its depths. Only those who have tasted the bitterness of despair know that there exists a solution for every complication. Every man remains in the last analysis the master of his fate. It is in the heart of the profound abyss that the strength of patience, the power of hope and the infinite means of salvation will be revealed to us.

Circumstances

Let us seek to attain that independence which leaves us free to watch, in joy, or in tears, but always calm and tranquil, the tragic or glorious procession of our life's events.

The Action of Man

Man is destined to the complete expansion of his faculties. As long as he feels latent forces within himself he will be restless and discontented; he may perhaps desire pleasure without pain, and make of faith a soft pillow for his laziness, but nothing can really satisfy him short of the absolute gift of himself.

His duty is to live, drawn by the mysterious current that moves all souls from one end of the universe to the other "without pause, without questioning, without the sense of having reached the goal; for truth progresses unceasingly. Nothing is certain, nothing stable, save faith in his course, the love of good, confidence in God. He must not allow himself to be bound by anything, for truth cannot exist in changeless dogma; truth is movement. He must have his part in all things and only keep what is pure, beautiful and beneficent. All the

The Understanding of Good

summits that life can offer must be scaled: love, science, art — till he gains a free horizon. For all is needful: doubt and faith, love and hate, sorrow and happiness — to build up in us the image of truth.... Progress is a series of deaths and resurrections. It is a chaos, a tragic mixture of good and evil; what matters the result if only the movement continues; what matters the error if the effort has left no stone unturned?

"What emerges from the fire is a new life, a tranquil force, and in the struggle man will refashion his religion, his life, his judgment; he will recreate himself."[1]

Those who do not understand that the supreme duty of man is to spend all the energy of which he is capable on every occasion that may be offered to him, cannot claim redemption. The worth of a human creature will always depend on the cost he is prepared to pay; and his progress will be proportionate to the strength of his effort. But in order to be truly efficacious the effort must become a habit.

A beautiful thought may add brilliancy to our spirit; but only a fine action can add force to our soul. With this principle as our basis, we

1 *Vie de Romain Rolland*, by Paul Seippel

The Action of Man

have the right to expect great things, for the present hour is only the dawn of a day when we shall pass from one great discovery to another still more marvelous.

Just as the child is ignorant of the power he will one day possess, so man only finds out by degrees the extent of his faculties; master even now of the ocean and the air, it will not be long before he penetrates the vaster regions of the mysterious unseen.

Thus the problem of destiny, which up to the present has been relegated to the domain of the fatal and irremediable, appears to us in quite another light. If we are convinced that each soul is a world wherein all the secrets of the universe are locked, and if we admit that man has almost unlimited power in that world, must we not realize that he can play a very considerable part in the destiny of that world — that is, in the individual's share of joy or sorrow?

Perhaps fate seems blind to us because we do not yet perceive the direct relation between the life of our soul and the events of our life. Most events take place because their germ is already in us. There are people whose future one

The Understanding of Good

can predict with certainty according to their character. God has willed that the happiness of man should lie partly in his own hands; and half of our worldly ills could be suppressed if man could only arrive at understanding and desiring good.

Sometimes the discovery of a microbe has sufficed to show us the means of ridding whole regions of infection, and the revelation of a single fault, recognized and conquered, can sometimes transform a man's life and reform a whole community. Surely then, a fuller knowledge of the means at our disposal will help us to take charge of our destiny.

This progress is the great work of the future; and even now we foresee the time when we shall act with greater power and more freely, in a larger field. But for the moment we are still held back by a chain of false ideas, accumulated through centuries of ignorance. Our hopes are too timid, our decisions too hesitating; they will linger short of achievement; but the men of tomorrow will profit by our efforts and succeed where we have failed.

What we have sown they will reap. With riper knowledge, they will know how to escape

The Action of Man

the weight of fruitless suffering and give true happiness a chance. They will not pursue, as we did, the phantom of illusory good, but will seek to realize the conditions of true good; they will be stronger and more healthy for they will have understood how to husband their strength for the propitious hours and the great issues.

The coming generation holds within it the triumph of human force, and our tired arms are outstretched toward it; we lay the last dream of our vanquished ideal at its feet. The coming generation will see the miracle of man; I say "miracle," because this recompense of good is a thing so unexpected to those who know life that it always appears to them as a miracle. But is not all happiness a miracle? And does the miracle lose its marvel because it is explained?

On the one hand, man has called what is only too often the clumsy or clever work of his own hand fatality or miracle; on the other, he has claimed for his own merit what he should have ascribed to God. It is undeniable that divine intervention is often interwoven with human intervention in the course of events; and man, while striving to acquire, should also open his hands to receive. Is this strange

The Understanding of Good

inexplicable gain a free gift or a deserved reward? We know not, but it seems that when man has reached a certain height he meets God there and is granted the privilege of working with Him. And so the discovery and the use of the complete faculties of man promise us a better future; but there is a limit to man's power; and the mortal, even at the highest level of his development, must pause; for earthly life resolves itself into a formidable question to which our world has no answer.

The Miracle of God

We have just made an appeal to the active powers of man; we have told him to fight, to assert himself, to will; now we feel the negation of action, we are in the presence of a mighty power which acts against the grain of our human ideas and manifests itself in proportion to our self-effacement. We must suppress action, put reason on one side and become silent, receptive, dependent. We must neutralize the human and make way for the superhuman — for the action of miracle. How can the man of action become passive, the wise man become as a child? There is a wisdom that strangely resembles innocence and a passivity which is not caused by want of energy, but is the outcome of the new life that rests on God.

In every struggle there comes a moment of exhaustion when the limit of human endurance imposes immobility on us; it is at

The Understanding of Good

this moment that divine intervention most frequently appears: "the miracle" which is at once the recompense of sovereign justice and the result of our own conscientious effort.

In order to reach us the miracle must often take strange forms; our deliverance does not only differ from what we had expected but produces unlooked-for results so that we seem suddenly to have undergone a change of soul. This phenomenon need in no way alarm us: it simply marks a new phase in our development. Let us try to understand and march on courageously.

In all that comes to us without provocation, prevision or desire on our part, we feel so strongly the action of a power foreign and superior to our own, that we instinctively assume, in the encounter of such events, a deferential and humble attitude. We actually regard the benefits that come to us by chance with much more confidence than we accord to those that result from our own efforts, and the undeserved gifts are the only ones to which we feel we really have a right.

In the depths of his own soul, the most incredulous man is so profoundly convinced

The Miracle of God

of the impotence of his own powers and the necessity for supernatural intervention that he relies unconsciously on what he calls the chances of "luck." Who has not known those hours, stripped of all resources, when the heart, still forced to hope, strains into the void, ready to wrest from the wind of chance the unexpected news that may restore the possibility of life? In spite of ourselves we live by miracles, and yet all the best that life has brought us, all that has enlarged our nature and transported our soul in an ecstasy of love and gratitude, has been the free gift of God.

How dear to me is that evening hour, full of languor and confidence, hope and renunciation, when the soul, born on the wings of dreamland, enters that paradise whose doors our spent powers have sought in vain to force! We have reached the limit of human order, of material law; we enter the realm of mystery, of infinitude; it is the hour when our own impotence leads us to hope for a divine and victorious intervention — it is the hour of miracle! The workman lays aside his tools, weary from the day's work; instead of hoped-for treasures he sees around him only broken ruins. But from the bottom of

The Understanding of Good

his humiliated heart rises a song of gladness, a memory of childhood: "Behold the fowls of the air ... consider the lilies of the field." God feeds them and gives them raiment. Surely He will think tenderly of man's fruitless efforts!

The defeat of our sage reason, our sturdy courage, has been foreseen by our soul, and the soul rejoices, for in this mortification it recognizes its triumph; man must abdicate if God is to manifest Himself. How good is that which He does, how deeply in accord with our true and intimate aspirations! How much better than anything we looked for! Let us pause. Silence. Here we are on the holy ground where, in one and the same thought, God and man may meet! Nothing in this triumph need make us proud. It is not a payment but a free gift. "Chance," says man. "The inexplicable," our heart tells us. And the vision of the invisible realities passes before our dazzled eyes. Suddenly we see, we understand, we adore, not a mere achievement, but a masterpiece, completed all unknown to us.

It is possible that, like a gifted painter who knows his palette well and has full command of his brush, we might arrive at creating a

The Miracle of God

picture of our life more or less corresponding to our glimpsed ideal, but we could never give it the radiance of life. There the greatest talent is helpless. God alone holds the secret of happiness.

A look, a word, a movement — all or nothing, according to whether God sends it to us at the right moment and in response to our inner aspiration. When we experience one of these moments of miracle we feel we are only poor artisans whose best efforts can but displace a little dust.

Barren Days

Life brings us days empty of all outward joy; around us is the desert! But within, unknown to us, the source of happiness remains intact. Why is it that at certain times this source of joy ceases to spring, leaving our soul to be consumed in anguish or be quenched in lethargic sleep? Have we been guilty of some fault of ignorance in spite of our goodwill, or has God thought it necessary for some reason we cannot grasp to abandon us to our weakness, forsaking our soul as He once forsook the soul of Jesus on the cross?

Be it as it may, we can no more escape from our inner privation than from our outward poverty when we have prayed, struggled and hoped, there remains nothing but to resign ourselves to humiliation and to await the possible intervention of God!

The only thing which can help us to live through these barren days is the thought that

The Understanding of Good

they must pass, as all that is human passes, and that some day hope will return to illuminate our life, just as the sun, after long days of mist, breaks through the clouds and lights up the horizon. Only then shall we realize that we have gone forward and that the days of gloom and seeming stagnation were in reality as the tunnel that takes the traveler to the other side of the mountain. We shall find ourselves again beneath other skies, amid new scenes, surely more favorable to our development and nearer to our true home. In that moment, when the newly rising sun discloses undreamed-of beauties, our soul is flooded with joy, and even the memory of past bitterness and tribulation will be wiped out.

The more frequently we experience these alternations of sadness and joy in our lives, the more steadfast will our faith become in the everlasting things, and we shall experience a more tireless patience toward the vexations and disappointments of daily life.

Success, or rather, happiness — for I will only speak here of inner realities — lasts only as long as we guard the spirit of sacrifice. But even the strongest and the best cannot always

Barren Days

escape the surprises of primitive nature, which at certain times claims its rights. Let us avoid severe judgment. Nature is an undisciplined child whose spirit we must not break, but rather seek to understand and guide with wisdom, humoring his imprudent whims. Let us beware of leading him into insincerity by demanding the impossible. We must remember that nothing is more vexatious than to believe oneself an angel when one is only a poor mortal. The far-seeing mother is not she who exacts the most from her child but she who best recognizes his possibilities.

We are not masters of the lights and shadows that pass over our soul, but we can at least welcome the splendor of the glad hours and courageously bear the darkness of the barren days.

To the Vanquished

Oh noble comforters, wherever your feet have trod on this earth, the ground is sacred and the work of your hands is blessed. Let all seek you whose wounds can be healed. Yet there is a threshold you cannot pass without sacrilege, for it leads to a sanctuary where only silence does not outrage — the scene of those mysterious sufferings that are forever inexplicable and incurable. You may deny it, but, alas, it exists, and its existence is the proof of its necessity; so we must accept it, even at the risk of disturbing our sense of justice, rather than seek to minimize the painful mystery by a lie. For suffering separated from all idea of merit or utility, suffering merely as such, will always remain the most profound and sacred enigma, before which all heads must bow.

It is truly a suffering that has no name, no meaning, no clear purpose — a suffering

The Understanding of Good

without truce and without end, which one endures, not because of the evil one has been guilty of, but through the virtue one has made one's own. It is not a sorrow that is content to grieve; far from it! It has sought a remedy everywhere — in man, in God, in action and in prayer, in embrace and in renouncement. But at the back of life it has felt death, and at the back of death the void.

Renunciation may appease the conscience for a while but it does not comfort the soul. Rather, it quenches it and renders it useless to others beneath the strain of a life without hope. Even if one is prepared to accept the fatal consequences of renunciation without understanding them, that renunciation is an affront to our conscience, which tells us to live. For only by living can we know truth. Only by living can we obey God, the same God who asks us to die. Today we must accept death in order to find deliverance; tomorrow that same deliverance can only be found by protest against death!

To live! We *must* live, but, Oh God, by what shall we live? By the flower that withers, the light that dies? To live: that is, to justify the thirst for happiness, to give rein to the

To the Vanquished

imagination, to awaken all the gods whom prudence had kept slumbering; to awaken them that they may tempt us toward the blue regions of the infinite that prove, on nearer sight, to be only implacable rocks against which all strength will be broken.

To live! What heroism that word stands for! To live! Compared with the effort life demands, death seems but the idle game of a child. Resignation may have its justification; it is but human, since we are weak and surrounded by enemies. But to blossom forth in gladness is superhuman; it is to contradict evidence, to affirm the unknowable, to will the impossible. Man may teach us how to die: God alone can sometimes enable us to live — to live, alas, without sustenance!

What countless elixirs man has invented to deliver suffering humanity from the torments of soul and body! But like so many poor invalids who have vainly tried all the remedies offered by science, numbers of suffering souls have followed in all sincerity the counsels of morality and religion without result.

To those whose bodies are undermined by disease, asylums are offered where they can end

The Understanding of Good

their days in peace; but for the sick souls there is neither refuge nor pity on earth: rejected by the disciples of joy, they are condemned by the worthy and respectable. "If they suffer, it is their own fault," say many. "Why can they not do as we do who have no sufferings?" Oh, cruel men with your narrow vision! No! even inscrutable suffering is not always a punishment; there are sufferings of which the cause and the purpose are equally unknown to man, sufferings that nothing can alleviate because their nature offers no ease but only teaches us to endure. In promising these sufferers deliverance in the name of God, perhaps you are acting contrary to God's will — that God who did not respond even to the cries of Calvary.

Those are not the impious whose prayers remain unanswered, whose efforts are without result and whose lives remain dark; the ways of God are mysterious, and the vanquished have their mission! Who knows if the creature, crushed and agonizing on the ground, from whom we turn away with that rather scornful pity we give to the cowardly and weak, has not spent more strength before acknowledging

To the Vanquished

himself vanquished than we have used to gain our victories?

When Jesus called the poor blessed he thought surely not only of those sorrows over which the spirit triumphs but also of the obscure heroes of those inner struggles which no victory has justified.

On the stony paths they have followed, the unfortunates have perhaps lost their faith in God, their love of their fellow creatures, their eternal hope; but they go on; and who shall say if the little, joyless steps they take in the gloom do not lead them more surely to the goal than our triumphal passage through the light?

The Courage to Doubt

The doubt of some skeptics is more worthy of admiration than the faith of certain believers, because it is proof of a more conscientious pursuit of a more disinterested truth.

There is a kind of doubt that only comes to those who have tried their strength to the utmost, and which the lukewarm will never experience; a doubt that is, perhaps, the supreme triumph of faith, for it proclaims the humility of the hero who is unconscious of his own glory.

One might almost affirm in a general way that only those who are too superficial to sound the depths of their soul, or too timid to explore the furthest limits of the horizon, escape the onslaughts of doubt.

Is it astonishing that no answer comes to the prayers of those who only pray with their lips? But when those whose prayer was the

The Understanding of Good

expression of absolute faith receive nothing, must they blame themselves? They know how they have prayed, and that their prayer deserves an answer. Must they doubt God? That is the wreck of faith in the name of sincerity. Terrible fall into the void! To be true, and dare to die for truth's sake — to lose, if need be, even eternity! Who will have such courage? The scoffer or the saint? He who cares not for truth, or truth's passionate disciple?

Doubt does not reject God: it rejects the odious caricature of a God whom it would fain have perfect. Doubt is the sign of the purest love, and he whose simple faith has never been deceived will remain ignorant of the highest conception of the divine, that which only a tried faith can reveal to him.

Doubt is the filter that purifies our faith, giving it a personal value which it would not otherwise have had. It is the ladder leading us painfully from earth to heaven, from the God of little children to the wise man's God.

Many lie to themselves and to life in order to keep their faith; but a soul that is strong, sincere and clear-sighted cannot live by falsehood; it must see all, know all and still

The Courage to Doubt

believe, if possible, in a greater truth which nothing that exists can destroy.

The greatest misfortune that can come to us is to lose the possibility of faith and hope. And yet God permits these trials. Doubt and despair are thus not always temptations which we must conquer but sometimes griefs we must endure.

Hope

Hope is the food of life; faith the sustenance of happiness. In order to be happy it suffices to believe and to wait; it matters little what we believe or await; true happiness is denied only to the skeptical and the indifferent.

In nature all things have their justification, the lowest perhaps being the most indispensable. The craving for happiness is an instinct as ineradicable as it is necessary; therefore we ought to understand it and cultivate it as a sacred gift confided to man by God.

Our soul is a sown field in which we are free to bring the seed of our choice to fruition. Too often the desire for happiness, that precious seed containing a whole harvest of fine virtues, is mistaken for a germ of egoism and ruthlessly destroyed.

In prompting us to aspire to a fuller existence, the desire for happiness keeps alive

The Understanding of Good

our will and the courage of effort. It is the spring of all our actions, thoughts and words – the axle on which turns the movement of terrestrial life.

The more a human being develops, the more intense his desire for happiness becomes; the exalted soul knows desires undreamed of by the mediocre. But this desire, like all the germs of good latent in us, demands cultivation: we must learn to believe in happiness, to will, and then to choose it.

Belief in happiness is not an illusion of youth, as is often assumed, but the experience of a force that grows and triumphs over reality. The more our feeble hope is flung and broken against the deceptions of life, the more surely will it rise powerful and transformed.

We suffer every time we doubt someone or something, but our sorrow is turned into joy as soon as we have recognized in that person or thing the immortal beauty that aroused our love. Doubt and disappointment are needed for the birth of true faith and genuine happiness; but for their continuance, confidence and hope are indispensable. Suffering is a means, happiness an end; and the danger is not in the actual doubt or

Hope

suffering but in the futile prolongation of these states through lack of energy and confidence in life. There are sorrows that awaken us because we are able to emerge from them, and others that crush us because we linger in them; we must know how to bear those that come to us from God and to cast off those that we so constantly bring upon ourselves.

Every trial has its good side; in the case of physical crisis we are led to discover the hidden treasures of the soul's life through the deprivation of outside interests; a moral crisis can enlarge our horizon and cause us to discover a higher truth with its saving grace. All sorrow, if we only know how to fathom it, ought to increase our happiness.

As the rhythm of breath maintains life, so the alternations of joy and sorrow, expanding and contracting our hearts, give life to the soul. To preserve the soul's health it is only necessary to purify the air we breathe and the impressions we receive; for there are not only fine joys and noble griefs but also petty pleasures and futile sorrows.

It is impossible to escape the sorrows inherent in life, but discouragement can be

The Understanding of Good

overcome equally with the bitterness, the hate or envy that make sorrow a menace to life: and it is possible to feed one's soul on pure joys and true happiness instead of offering it mediocre satisfactions and uncertain joys.

The ardent desire for happiness urges man toward vice or virtue. This desire, just and legitimate in principle, may, under the influence of tendencies of a vexatious kind, swerve and produce a preference for the gross pleasures of egoism rather than the pure joys of love; but even then it does not merit suppression. To stifle desire, hope or joy in a human being is always to diminish his vital force and reduce his chance of true happiness. The bird whose wings have been cut lest it should escape will lose at the same time its sense of joyous transport. So we must not repress the longing for happiness but learn to distinguish between its different forms. The child, whose judgment is not formed, must be taught to discern the value of the things that surround him so that he may be able to choose the most beautiful.

Life undertakes to raise the ideal of happiness for any human creature who has but sufficient goodwill, by allowing him to test

Hope

the inadequacy of all that is mediocre. Before desiring the kingdom of God the apostles looked to the advantages of an exclusively earthly rule; and these aspirations, refined and developed by use, rendered them capable of realizing the higher happiness that comes with the possession of spiritual benefits.

Yet life — in other words, circumstances — does not undertake to educate our taste unaided; our will must collaborate with life, not the active will which is the privilege of well-balanced natures but the will possessed by even the feeblest, the simple assent or spontaneous adherence of the spirit to preexistent good. There is no question of effort here: to accomplish good, effort is necessary; to love it, we need only recognize it. If I have grasped the beauty of altruism, I shall naturally place myself in its protecting shelter. Christians call this choice "conversion." Thenceforth, altruism will undertake to teach me, to help me to judge, speak and act so that my first impulse in the presence of men and things will be a generous gesture. The same is true of benevolence, courage, sincerity — all the qualities that constitute human perfection; it is only by loving

The Understanding of Good

them that one finally arrives at their possession. If they are forced they have no vitality; their whole existence depends on their becoming natural, spontaneous, inherent in our true self.

We must learn to see the beautiful; the rest will follow without effort, for we always end by resembling what we admire. Admiration is the only efficacious education. Our desire for happiness, really a nascent desire for good, must follow the same course. When experience has proved how incapable honors, pleasure and prosperity are of giving us happiness, we shall seek higher and better things: satisfactions for the spirit and the heart; art, science; and these in their turn, failing to satisfy, will lead us on to the discovery of the central and creative joy, the happiness of the gods.

Man is born to create; in creating he becomes himself, accomplishes his destiny. His whole life is only an initiation into the creative power.

To create is not merely to produce a work; it is to give out one's own individuality. Man becomes a creator when, after the innumerable stages of adaptation to alien influence, he finally grasps what is really his own, what he receives

Hope

not from men but directly from God as a special personal message. Thus the philosopher is further advanced than the man dependent on material good, and the artist even further than the philosopher because he aims at an even more personal result. The philosopher climbs painfully to the summit; the poet is transported thither on the wings of genius; inspiration reveals to him what the philosopher discovers by arduous labor. Yet, arriving by different routes and led, the one by wisdom, the other by his muse, they meet on the same height, from whence they can together contemplate the divine.

The possession of lasting happiness, which must constitute our interior capital, does not in any way exclude the desire and the utility of passing joys; if it exists without them they are still necessary if it is to remain real and vital. It is in spending one's treasure that one best realizes its value. If the beauty I see in my hours of solitude ravishes my soul, my rapture will be more intense when it is shared, and I shall never create better than when I do so for love of some human creature and under the influence of that love.

The Understanding of Good

True happiness is not to be found outside life; it does not hover above as the sky hovers over the earth; it is *in* life, it is life itself — full life, with all of its heroic struggles and sublime joys.

Happiness is not a reflection thrown on us by our surroundings; it is a radiance that emanates from us, resting on all we touch and giving to all things again the life we draw from them. Nonetheless, if exterior joys are but the mirrors reflecting the deeper happiness within us, it is well that in the hours of weariness their bright image should sometimes assure us that we are happy.

The more fully we have grasped the reality of true happiness, the more susceptible we shall become to the humble joys of everyday life. So smiles the child at the toys and treats placed within its reach.

Joy is the purest of all the springs that gush in the depths of our hearts; it murmurs the sweet, clear melodies of life that soften with their charm the austere chords of profound truth.

Why make of life only a duty when we have the power to make it a joy? Why force nature to conventional molds when we can

Hope

so safely leave her to her own spontaneous expansion? In obeying the laws of their nature the blossoming flower and the playing child know by instinct that which we discern with difficulty, after questioning the centuries and weighing the worlds; and the happiness I take as it passes because I love it and it seems beautiful to me, will bring wisdom to my heart while filling it with light.

But life has lost its power to teach us because instead of accepting it as it is, in simplicity of heart, we have deliberately made of it a painful and unwholesome riddle.

Happiness is repose, not effort; it is by allowing comforting, luminous, tender impressions to have access to us and not by struggle to conquer them that the soul develops and expands. We may hope for all from life, but we must always hope for what we love best, and love what seems to us most beautiful. Such hope is never a fantasy, since we know that life is infinite and that the wonderful has a more real existence than the mediocre.

Belief in happiness is the immortal crown of life. If disappointments and sorrows were able to wrest it from us, they would take away

The Understanding of Good

the best we have, but they would only pluck the petals. The flowers of happiness do not grow in the moist and perfumed soil of spring days but from the arid ground of sorrow. They have their roots in the bowels of the earth and they will blossom again with the first warm days.

If I can extract a fine happiness from some poor joy that hardly makes another smile, do I not owe it to sorrow? Nothing shines with such a radiance as the joy of the vanquished; I would rather savor the joyous moment of the unhappy than share the happy hours of the fortunate, for his ray comes to him direct from heaven and brings all heaven to me, while the brightness of the fortunate comes from the earth and can only light up a single ridge.

Whatever the black phantoms of our despairing hours may tell us, we are moving toward life and not death — to the life that gradually casts off its mortal garments and dons its imperishable vesture. Therefore, we must not renounce our possessions as those who prepare for death, but, adorning ourselves for life, seek to acquire all we still lack by hearkening humbly, as little children, to the voice of true wisdom.

Hope

Clearly, our solitude must increase with the growth of our ideal; but our capacity for happiness grows too, and thus our soul, enriched, may even in the autumn of life taste those joys denied it in its young spring.

Nothing is so personal as happiness; each soul is fitted for a joy entirely individual; often a whole life is required to discover it; for it is more difficult to surrender ourselves to the inner gods of whose presence none save ourselves are conscious, than to adapt our souls to the conventional forms of happiness.

And yet how often our happiness, hardly grasped, is snatched from us! We must learn to discover and love other joys, for it is better to live maimed than not to live at all; and surely the courage that helps the lame man to walk is a higher testimony to life than the victorious step of one who knows no hindrance.

To live is one form of suffering; to die, another; but life is a fruitful suffering and death a sterile one.

Let us not fear ambitious dreams: we ought to expect much of life, since we are made for happiness. Our striving after the ideal will rise to the height of our dreams, just as the water

The Understanding of Good

of the fountain must reach its true level. The water of the fountain springs from a powerful jet and rises toward heaven; but, checked by the weight of the atmosphere, it disperses and falls in a thousand fructifying drops on the barren earth. And so effort rises and is split up, but through its own check it develops qualities useful to humanity. To seek to rise heavenward and to fall to earth — that is our destiny; but, in falling, to help others to live, to desire, and in their turn, to rise.

To hold imprisoned in our soul a torrent of life and to guard it from overflowing or becoming exhausted; this is our duty, a formidable duty that demands no small measure of wisdom and strength.

Our Disappointments

There are those who hold that because disappointments are inherent in life we must not take them too tragically. And, indeed, how easily the majority of men accept mediocrity! Success, and not failure, surprise them. So possibly they give less proof of their courage than of their incapacity to entertain high hopes and noble dreams.

For the higher natures, whose tastes and habits have been turned since childhood toward the beautiful, who believe in the possibility of realizing their inner ideals, resignation is more painful; a disappointment is always a disturbing problem to them and may even appear to be an irreversible disaster.

The noble soul believes instinctively, and because it believes it gives; it gives without reserve, not time, strength, devotion, but its sacred treasure, the best of itself, the intimate and tender benevolence of supreme hours.

The Understanding of Good

All this it gives as one who gives his life to save the life of another. And having given he is left with nothing, for in giving he has spent himself for others. Yet never has he felt himself so rich, for to him it is more precious than life to see the rebirth and unfolding of a soul.

He has believed, not blindly, not holding the object of his faith faultless, but simply because a day comes when one must believe without reserve and give without restraint. This is the price of the soul's true life.

Through all the raptures and the agonies of that complete offering, the immutable purpose, the widening of our life, persists. This sacred and tragic gift is the condition necessary for a higher morality; to shrink from it would be to deny to gold the purifying fire.

To be worthy is, after all, more important than to be happy. It is the entire gift of Himself — a gift possibly misunderstood — that established the glory of Jesus. And we shall see the growth of our soul only in proportion to the measure in which we hazard its purest essence. The prudent man may keep what he has got; the gambler only has the chance of making his fortune.

Our Disappointments

Yet though high ambitions urge us to launch our barque boldly on the sea of noble impulse, risking the loss or gain of all, wisdom offers us a means of saving our faith from the wreck of our dreams.

By obeying the secret command which insists on complete giving, the soul proves its capacity for obedience and greatness; by and during the ruin of its dreams in conflict with reality, it shows its faith and courage; a last lesson remains to be learnt, that of wisdom, which can discern the true value of things.

It is not so much a question of suffering less as of avoiding unproductive pain; not of loving less, but of better knowing those we love, in order to avoid the double error of asking what they cannot give and offering what they are incapable of receiving.

Discernment does not diminish love but rather illuminates it, for it teaches love to understand the quality of its gifts and how to apportion them according to the needs of others.

If love were of necessity blind, it would be only a snare; but it is the supreme good that comprehends more fully through clear vision, and loves more deeply as compassion

The Understanding of Good

grows. The soul should know what it gives and to whom it gives; it must also know what it possesses and what are its secret stores.

The word "disappointment" implies the harm done to us by others; but let us also think about the part we have ourselves played in our disappointments. Thus, in certain dissolutions, the grief of lost affection is mixed with poorer sentiments, injury to our self-love, humiliation, possibly envy — the usual attendants of that unhappiness which has not yet shaken off the fetters of egoism. This dross will fall away as love becomes purified; and the soul will rise up after the sacrifice, ennobled and heroic for all time.

To give is a joy. Those who give in order to gratify themselves are far more numerous than those who give to comfort others. The need of giving is often a sign of weakness and egoism, whilst the power to refuse implies a spirit of sacrifice and self-control.

It is not necessary to be constantly giving; and we should give only to those who need — fewer than one imagines. Those are rare who know how to receive. We must not give to all who beg, for many do so from habit, with no

Our Disappointments

intention of elevating themselves. And we must not give because our heart overflows, but when the need of others demands our aid; not because we are rich, but because they are poor.

God never asks for our excess but demands what is necessary to us. For, though giving is a joy, it is a joy that implies sacrifice. If we are disappointed, it is because we have given wrongly; the unselfish giver need never fear ingratitude: it cannot reach him.

What is disappointment? The pain we experience at the failure to find what we look for in people and things. Are they then to blame for being what they are? No! In any case, not in their relation to us. The fault is ours for having failed to understand and see them as they are.

We shall always meet with disappointment until we are able to free ourselves from egoism. We are there for others and God is there for us. So let us not occupy our minds with receiving but only with giving.

To give does not always mean to give oneself. It is possible to give by remaining passive, by refusing, even by taking away; the most excellent gift is that of a constant patience. All that we do, even unconsciously, to enrich,

The Understanding of Good

comfort, and ease the suffering of others, is a gift — the only gift that can never disappoint.

Let us know how to distinguish the real from the apparent value of the joys and sorrows life brings us; we shall thus learn to control our feelings and to retain our moral equilibrium.

The urgent need of affection in tender hearts often renders them liable to attach too much importance to feelings; not that these feelings are insincere, but because they are weak and incapable of fulfilling our expectations. When such an affection meets with shipwreck, let us not allow our vital force to be consumed by pain and regret.

The power to descend to the depths of the soul is not always the sign of a profound soul; there are those who, though gifted with clear comprehension and high ideals, lack strength. They dream of, feel, and rhapsodize over the ideal, but they do not live it; only its reflection shines on them. Alas for one who relies on them; he will drink the bitter cup of disillusion to the dregs. We must believe them, for they are sincere; help them, for they are weak; but we must never lean on them. Incapable of action, they betray themselves at the first difficulty,

Our Disappointments

and fail you, not through lack of affection, but lack of endurance. To such characters one must give unceasingly and never ask. They cannot help themselves: their powers of devotion are as cramped as limbs that have never been used. As soon as we beg a service from them they regard us with a surprise akin to terror, as if dreading a trial far beyond their strength, and they search for any excuse that will enable them to escape from us.

We have erred, first, in asking of them what they are unable to give, and then, more gravely, in reproaching them for not having given it; finally, and this time, fatally, in despairing over a disappointment which a little wisdom would have shown us to be inevitable.

We must never allow circumstances to exhaust our heart; let us instead vigorously defend it against bitterness and discouragement. And if we must sacrifice a joy, let us at least cling to the blessing it brought us in the enhancement of our inner life.

However profound our knowledge of the human heart may be, it does not always suffice to save us from pitfalls. Even the wisest are

The Understanding of Good

sometimes deceived and are obliged to pass through the hard school of misplaced love.

It is relatively easy to give oneself, for the soul is thus only obeying its natural inclination, fulfilling its true destiny, moving toward happiness; it is a spontaneous action demanding neither wisdom nor will nor courage. But to reassert one's self-ascendancy involves violence to Nature and a movement in the direction of unhappiness. This action calls for the greatest effort of which we are capable.

Weak natures wear themselves out; they can never take back what they have given of themselves because they are incapable of the voluntary action demanded by reason; they only know the forced action imposed by fate. And so they shut their eyes to reality and let themselves be beguiled by falsehood. They refuse to see until the day when, in revolt and bitterness, they would vent all their spite on the object of the sacrifice which has been demanded of them. But to recover possession of one's soul does not mean revolt; it is the renunciation of self-abandonment, resistance to the tendernesses of a heart rendered perhaps too emotional; the return to a more austere way

Our Disappointments

of life, and thenceforth to seek support only in the innermost refuge of one's own soul.

This renewal of complete self-possession ought not to be an act of vengeance but of the highest reason; it should not be made at the expense of the one from whom we have withdrawn ourselves, but rather in his interests. We have no desire to punish him but to put an end to his exploitation of us. We resign the joys of love but not its obligations.

Only he can regain the mastery of his soul who truly possesses himself, who does not depend entirely on his feelings, however precious they may be to him, but on the steady radiance of the sanctuary of which his love was but a single ray.

The quality of love does not depend on the one who inspires it but on him who feels it. If love has been withdrawn from you, there is nothing astonishing or humiliating to you in this change, for it is not your merit which was insufficient but the soul's force of him who loved you.

Certain human creatures, without moral or physical beauty are nevertheless loved, because chance has thrown in there path a soul

The Understanding of Good

capable of a strong emotion. Others, favored with the highest gifts, meet with treachery and desertion.

But the joy that love has given you — perhaps only a simple illusion of brief duration — has nonetheless been happiness, and will bring to you who have known it the same recompense as a truer felicity.

What matters it whether our steps be on the sand or the rocks, if only they have led us to the summit from whence we can command a wider horizon and breathe a purer air?

Happiness does not come to us from human creatures but from God, who sends it through the divine element in us. And the more there is of this divinity in our soul, the greater will be our capacity for happiness. We shall be loved and understood in vain by a chosen spirit if our faculties do not allow us to realize our privilege.

When the love that gave us delight forsakes us, let us not bear a grudge against the weakness of him who has robbed us of it, but rather bless the Master of all happiness for having deigned to accord us a share of that delight. The quality of our happiness is not changed because its cause was less worthy, and the memory of it

Our Disappointments

loses none of its beauty for having been based on an illusion. It is we who tarnish a gracious and noble memory by our petty grievances of injured self-love and disappointed ambitions. We must accept happiness as a glorious summer day whose advent we cannot explain and whose duration is uncertain, but by which, while it lasts, we are warmed and fortified. Let us be grateful for the free and unexpected gift.

Happiness or love has revealed to us the kernel of inner strength; had they lingered too long, might they not have weakened us and turned us from our essential purpose: the initiation into the high joy of the wise? For the end and aim of happiness is not to bring us transports of delight, but through rapture to raise us to a larger conception of beauty!

Let us never seek the why and wherefore of joy or sorrow: none will answer us. Even those who were the harbingers of our glad and tragic days can tell us nothing. If we ask them and they are kind, they will smile or weep at the consequences of their involuntary intervention in our destiny; if they are egoists they will pass on and think no more of it. You, therefore, who are wise, turn not to men, to bless or denounce

The Understanding of Good

them, but look above and beyond them to the universal destiny; for it knows all and is ever at hand to enlighten us.

We must be able to strengthen our soul as we do our body, to bear an intense and inevitable pang without wincing. Even as we are able to train our body to endure all winds and weathers, so can we also fortify our soul to bear all sorrows without despair.

Fraud

We live in the reign of hypocrisy. It has penetrated all things: science, politics, industry, art, morality and religion. The very air we breathe is infected; the universe we behold is merely a semblance. Men deceive themselves by repressing their true aspirations. They deceive each other in professing wealth, happiness and feelings which they have not. They seek to deceive God by a false worship.

Side by side with the fraud that rules the world of egoism exists a graver fraud that invades the sanctuary and endangers the sacred objects of our affections and our beliefs; the fraud practiced by honest folk, friends of virtue, and in the supposed interests of virtue. And in the midst of this chaos, the soul, unable to live except by truth, seeks in vain a spot wherein to find solace for its weary yearning.

The Understanding of Good

Truly, one of the greatest wrongs we can do the cause of good is to lower it to the level of the first-comer. As well might we gild a marble of Michelangelo, thinking to enhance its value, as we attempt to flatter good in order to make it more attractive in the eyes of those who shrink from its austerity.

Good is an established value which vulgar flattery can only diminish; the proselytes thus gained are only mercenaries. Truth must live naked, or it is naught; forsaken, it still pursues its end — the assertion of absolute beauty. If there are two things eternally irreconcilable, they are good and falseness. Good may assume all forms but one — semblance. A sincere vice is nearer truth than a fictitious virtue.

If, for sincere souls, the discovery of falseness in the world is one of the most tragic of all experiences, to find it in the sacred domain of the divine is a mortal blow. It is not so much the evil openly displayed that disgusts the honest heart, as the well-meaning traffic carried on by the zealots of virtue. They spoil the market by selling at a low price pearls whose value they ignore, simply in order to please the public taste of those with shallow

Fraud

purses. They obstruct the pathway of the ideal by propagating semi-virtues, divided spirits and lukewarm souls. What value to gain legions if no individual is stirred? To fill churches with empty souls?

We do no service to a fellow creature by placing at his disposal a virtue he does not desire, whose meaning he knows not and in the practice of which he has never tested his powers; for he will always end by finding its weight too heavy for his shoulders; he will hasten to rid himself of it forever, and in that false experience he will lose even the inclination toward good, which, without prodding, might have naturally sprung up in his heart. Nothing is so fatal as to reject virtue and to be disillusioned by duty. Judas thought he would find success by enlisting as Christ's disciple; he was mistaken, and his disappointment in realizing the austerity of good was the cause of his infamy. It is more serious than one imagines to persuade anyone to follow the straight path.

Let us be straightforward in good above all; first and foremost just because it is good; for it is preferable never to make a single proselyte than to expose one soul to the irrevocable

The Understanding of Good

consequences of a disillusionment in the matter of faith.

No, good will not reward you with the gains you look for. She is a sovereign who demands free service from noble knights. All those who seek recompense from good will be disappointed.

I know that one associates the smile of unchangeable benevolence with certain ideals of saintliness, the sign and seal of the perfect blessedness of the soul. I have often seen these smiles but I have never believed them. True happiness is solemn, discreet and silent; it suffices to itself, as does all that is profound; it has no need to seek external favor.

Virtue is an act of heroism and supreme unselfishness, to which many aspire but few achieve. It has but one reward, only one — freedom: it bestows the tranquil certainty of a strength that has triumphed and that thenceforth can never be shaken; out of the slave it makes a king.

Why wish to appear better than one is? The worth of a soul depends much less on the number of its virtues than on its sincerity. A truly great soul is one that dares to be honest

Fraud

equally in its defects as in its good qualities. Does not the frank avowal of our faults raise us to the dignity of the faultless?

The desire for good is an excellent thing, but it would be rash to confuse it with the realization of good. To desire it we need only a well disposed heart; but a long-tried heart alone can make it live.

Thus I may desire renunciation, may voluntarily deprive myself of what is pleasant and conquer all the revolts and discouragements of my suppressed nature so as to assist the development of this virtue. Shall I thereby have learned renunciation? No! But if in the course of my life I find out that the things I craved have lost, in possession, the worth they seemed to have, I cease to yearn for them and detach myself quite naturally. This renunciation is not merely a dream of my goodwill, but a reality experienced; it is part of me. And so it is with other virtues; though we may have longed for them times without number, we only possess those we have lived.

I remember once discovering the full beauty of truth in the deep glance of a child's eyes. The look condemned nothing, desired nothing,

The Understanding of Good

knew nothing; it came from the infinitely pure regions of primitive nature, with all of its wisdom and kindness; wherever it rested, light glowed; evil did not flee beneath the beams of its tranquil transparency as before a judge, but the evil-doer became good, for suddenly he too understood. Beneath that look it would have been impossible to lie, not because our disloyalty would have been guessed — those eyes could not see anything that was ugly — but because their clarity absorbed all shadows. Yet it was not the glance of an angel; the child had faults, but it knew how to be true in good as in evil, in its love as in its anger, in word and in movement; its beauty was the reflection of that perfect sincerity before which all must bow, since it is the reflection of the divine.

In our deeds as in our soul, nothing can endure that is based on a lie. Even had we all the virtues under the sun, we can only be good and joyous when we are sincere; and our actions can only be productive and beautiful if they spring from deeply felt inner experience.

Modern life, so essentially superficial, fighting shy of effort and fed by shallow

Fraud

sentiment, offers us only artificial creations that excite our senses but cannot nourish our souls.

We shall not create original or productive art by the chance encounter of passing emotions whose image we may reproduce more or less faithfully, but by giving ourselves for what we are and seeking to be worth much in order that we may give much.

How many people live in falsehood which they recognize but have not the courage to renounce!

Sincerity is the touchstone by which we can appraise the moral value of a man. In some natures the need of truth is so urgent that they know no peace till they have tested all things for themselves. But great power and resolute faith are needed to withstand the disillusion that follows a profound investigation of life. Only after having passed through all doubts and having faced the great void, will the passionate worshipers of truth find at last that inner truth which alone can satisfy the fierce demands of their souls.

In order to avoid the contagion of lies and recover our true nature — that nature lying at the core of every heart, though few will admit

The Understanding of Good

it — we must have the courage to see ourselves as we really are. We must, if only for a moment, cast off the artifice we mistake for our veritable self, the self we believe necessary to our well-being while in reality it is our chief hindrance. Let us tear off the mask and show ourselves as in truth we *are*, as we should be were we not obliged to consider others or explain ourselves in any way — as we are when no one is by, as we were in our childhood. And when once we have found this virgin soil let us cultivate it, for only there can the roots of our virtues sprout and all joys break into blossom.

Good should be a spontaneous act, achieved without effort, as the act of breathing results from the fact of being alive.

In order to grow, effort is necessary; in order to do good it is enough to let our new self live. This good does not tire us, it comforts, as the blooming of the flower completes the destiny of the plant. It can shine perpetually with undimmed radiance because its source is an inner reality and a natural abundance.

Studied good, on the contrary, demanding as it does a continual effort, calling on us to say and do things we believe ought to be said and

Fraud

done, but which do not respond to any inner need, wearies us because it is based on pretense and not on reality.

This good may dazzle for a moment, like the spark produced by the shock of the elements; it can never give us the quiet glow, unconscious and harmonious, of the radiance shed by God Himself.

Such studied good not only fatigues but also constitutes a great danger for us: it blinds us to our own defects and spreads unconscious hypocrisy in the world.

To avoid this pitfall, so common in our day of unduly forced virtue, we must first of all give up our conception of good in the form of a certain ideal and then rid ourselves of the habit we have acquired of seeking to copy this ideal.

Let us no longer busy ourselves with thinking of what we ought to be in order to imitate the gestures of this ideal, but seek to know what we *are*, and to live it.

We shall possibly obtain a result less in conformity with our ideal. But it will be something stronger and more beautiful, since it will be more true.

Exceptions

The source of dishonesty is not always a lack of sincerity in the heart. There are certain very sincere people who, full of good intentions, lie through excess of imagination (this is frequently the case with children), through negligence, fear, and even necessity. This forced lying, the most tragic of all forms of dishonesty, is the result of the severity and narrowness of human judgments.

Indeed, how is it possible to be true when one is not free? And how can freedom exist in a community where every activity of life is labeled in advance? If your truth has the good fortune to be adaptable to one of the current models, it is accorded the right to live; but if it does not fit into any of the customary frames, it is condemned either to silence, thus tacitly pretending to be what it is not, or to a misrepresentation of its real language in order that the public may have access to it. Thus,

The Understanding of Good

purest intentions suffer distortion through the influence of the environment in which they manifest themselves. Only the ingenious, or those too coarsely grained to realize the effect they produce, can be sincere with immunity.

The impossibility of making themselves understood on the one hand, and on the other the fear of condemnation, forces certain natures to deceive. And is not this fear often only too well justified? One desires to be sincere, but one must reckon with one's strength. There are burdens the bravest man ought not to take upon himself, lest he sink under them. The truth that would expose a weak and sensitive nature to a scorn he is unable to bear is an error and a wrong.

The lies which have their source in a want of natural strength are as equally excusable as those which certain social conditions force on us; for in both cases the true authors of the fraud are not those who lie but those who condemn without understanding. As long as we are not wise enough to realize our own ignorance, or charitable enough to empathize with the difficulties of others, there will inevitably be liars on earth. Our spirit has been so laden with rules and maxims it has lost the

Exceptions

power of natural and impulsive judgment; it no longer estimates a man by his individuality but according to an accepted standard.

We have a mania for comparing and generalizing, but God has not created things in relation to each other but in relation to an invisible truth which we do not comprehend; the rule does not exclude the exception but there are exceptions that annul the rule. The abnormal, as well as the normal, has its place in the vast complex of truth; and if this seems strange to us it is surely because of our own shortness of vision.

There are many things in the moral and material domains which we cannot understand, but none save egoism which we have the right to despise. A careful scrutiny of what we were about to reject as doubtful will show us a thousand mysterious and revealing doors opening into the great unknown.

At the root of all contempt is vanity; and the zeal we display in reforming humanity often only serves to trumpet our own virtues. Hearts are diverse; diverse too, the truth lying in each heart. However clear-sighted we may be, we shall never see more than an infinitesimal

The Understanding of Good

part of it. Even the most all-embracing justice cannot see all; there are cases outside all law. As in every temple there exists a sanctuary consecrated to mystery, so should there be in every soul a niche for the inexplicable; only so can the soul keep its balance in the immense whirlwind of conflicting influences.

Instead of proclaiming justice from some summit, let us follow the obscure paths where the humble dwellings of the despised stand, and try to understand the part their ignorance has played in their misfortune, and how their disabilities have led them into falsehood. We should not act and judge according to preconceived ideas, generally false, but seek simply to aid, to understand and to love.

Ah! If only humanity could understand, or failing that, abstain from pronouncing judgment; how many hearts would open! — how many lives unfold and consciences assert themselves! Delivered from the yoke of our uncompromising absolutism, the despised would venture at last to tell us the secret of their maimed souls. They would teach us to see more clearly, to understand more deeply and to love more wholly.

The Patience that Endures

Creation is composed of a collection of existing forces that grow and find their equilibrium in mutual sustenance. Without the earth that bears the tree, the branch that cradles the nest, our forests would have remained empty and silent. And, in the moral sphere, our souls cannot form or our virtues develop except on a basis of mutual patience.

The virtue by which we are able to bear with one another rests, like everything else that is true, upon a sacrifice; all contact between men presupposes an effort, often pain, which none can escape save at the price of narrowing his horizon and hardening his heart.

There is a legitimate solitude where our soul, yearning for communion with the infinite, has the right to retire; and another, a selfish solitude which is only the refuge of our cowardice.

Patience is a passive quality, scarcely appreciated by the world, which only recognizes

The Understanding of Good

forces capable of producing an obvious effect. And yet, to obtain a victory, we need the cooperation of our passive qualities equally with that of the active ones. It is not possible to have talent without perseverance, authority without abnegation, courage without self-control. A passive quality, growing as it does in silence, requires longer for its development than an active one, stimulated constantly by visible progress.

The worth of a quality is to be measured by its sincerity, but its strength is only appreciable by its durability. Of all the virtues, patience demands the longest and most sustained effort.

The art of patiently bearing is a force that grows in us according to the measure in which we learn to get outside ourselves and to understand others — to widen our scope of vision. It is the wisdom that smiles at small things and worries only over those that are worthy of emotion. It is that tact able to seize the appropriate moment and discern the intentions of others as well as their words or deeds. It is the wisdom that enables one to spare the weak and withstand all storms.

The Patience that Endures

The art of bearing with others is the benevolence that takes from his brother the last drop in his cup of sorrow, that removes the stone from his pathway to keep him from stumbling, that finds the right word and can also keep silent, that is ready always to take upon itself the burden at hand.

This burden bearer is a silent hero; he is never a defender of evil but always the champion of good; we do not feel his presence and yet he is active everywhere; humanity may seem to dispense with him, but in reality it is he who, in sustaining humanity, helps it to live.

Patience is the great agent of peace. Like mortar, it holds together all the stones of the social edifice; in the world, in the family, wherever human beings are called upon to live together. Even were they perfect and profoundly attached to each other, their life would be mutual torture without patience. We really owe to this virtue the best we possess on earth: the possibility of being with one another, of understanding and loving one another.

The virtue of patience is acquired in small quantities, from sacrifice to sacrifice, and it finally renders us capable of bearing even

The Understanding of Good

permanently, a burden ten times greater than our natural strength could carry.

Many people regard humanity as something from which they wish to profit; others wish to reform it; but humanity only asks to be born with. We are not called upon to judge men but to live amongst them in purity and love; for only by bearing with them as they are can we give them the opportunity of becoming what they can be.

But can one really change a soul? Those who are dishonorable generally remain so all their lives, however fine may be the example they have before them; all we can do for them is to prevent them from harming themselves and others and to hope that their bleak experience of life may be blessed with light. Those who are noble remain noble under circumstances and influences of the most unfavorable kind; they are noble even in their errors, thus proving how true it is that our real worth lies far from the visible world of our actions.

We shall influence humanity in proportion to our understanding of it and our capacity to bear with it courageously.

The Patience that Endures

Among the characters we are called on to meet with in life we find benevolent souls sent by God like rays from a brighter land; but we also meet disturbing personalities whom I should describe as alien, contradictory and mendicant souls.

The *alien* souls are those who, differing from us in their essence, cannot come into contact with us. The barrier between us is similar to that between people of different tongues. The obstacle is in a sense material — a wall all the more unscalable because it has not been voluntarily raised. Were we to share the whole of life with these beings, to embrace them a thousand times, no real communion would be possible. In the presence of an alien soul we must abandon all attempts at giving, and resign ourselves to being useless. The wisest course of all would be to avoid them, for nothing is so burdensome as the weight of an existence whose vibration one cannot share, of a love that cannot unfold.

Contrary souls are in one sense less difficult to tolerate than alien souls; for far from condemning us to inaction, they call forth all the moral intelligence of which we are capable.

The Understanding of Good

Here it is not a question of sitting down in resignation at the foot of an inexorable barrier but of using all our energy to raise about ourselves a protecting rampart without which we should always be in danger of attack, and a thousand times on the brink of being disarmed. The contrary souls dispose of an infinite variety of means to provoke us, to wound our sensibilities and ignore our treasures. Their attacks are directed with so much precision and subtlety, as well as candid ease, it is hardly possible to ascribe them only to human malevolence. If we look closely into things, we are obliged to admit that their arrows drawn less in the intent to harm than merely for amusement are the ones that most successfully reach their target. So we must not blame them, but the mysterious powers with which a demon or a god has infected them in order to harm or to test us. Our human weapons cannot deflect their malign darts; only the divine shield can deaden their blows.

There are beings whose energy is so antagonistic to our own that their presence alone suffices to trouble our interior harmony, preventing us literally from breathing and

The Patience that Endures

spreading our wings for flight to the higher regions.

If our knowledge of the soul's life were more enlightened, the errors that condemn beings so dissimilar to a shared life would be unthinkable! But while we await these better times, let us bear with even the unbearables, and do so without becoming hard or despairing — cherishing for our soul the hours of relaxation and relief. Let us know how to sometimes close the doors and windows and only show our façade, decorated as attractively as possible; for in certain characters the need to torment is often only a subconscious need for excitement in life, and their blows are neutralized if they fall on a surface of indifference.

In the presence of contradictory souls the secret to bearing with them lies in a profound sense of justice; we must, in the troubles they bring to us know how to reckon with their irresponsibility. In ceasing to be upset with them, we dissipate the bitterness and irritation so often present in the practice of patience.

There are other souls who only approach us in order to receive: they are the *mendicant* souls. With an open heart and a hand always

The Understanding of Good

outstretched, these souls make a constant call on our devotion and sympathy — on all the forces in us and even on powers we do not possess. And when at last, convinced of their misery, moved by their sorrows, we are ready, in an excess of noble disinterestedness, to sacrifice all in order to comfort them, they turn away to seek sympathy from another or, absorbed by some sudden interest, they forget even the existence of the treasures we have renounced for their sake.

These souls are especially dangerous because they appeal to our inner desire, which is to give, and because they have the power to move us. We give to them so naturally; how can we do otherwise in the face of their great need and their beseechings? If they are to be believed, their life is saved each time we help them; and who is not flattered at the thought of having saved a life? And they are right; one *does* save their life, but only to see it lost again tomorrow!

It is not hard to discover these beggar souls: just pour out to them, in your turn, your own needs, your fatigues, and at once you will see them withdraw, not through want of

The Patience that Endures

understanding — they understand all — but through their incapacity to make an effort to help you. Such egoism revolts you, you decide to abandon them; an error, for it would be unjust. You must take people as they are, but dream no longer of counting on them in the future; let them, on the contrary, count on you; go on giving, but in small portions, without giving of *yourself*; do not let yourself be repaid either in words or tears but realize that much in them is only morbid exaltation. Take them seriously, for they are much to be pitied, but never tragically, for their pain is only fleeting; and rely on time to remedy things which for the moment may seem irremediable.

How numerous they are, these poor creatures without force or will, who scour the world on their errands of mendicancy, begging from everyone a cure for the incurable malady of life which we are all called on, alas, to bear alone.

The effort of our life will not have been in vain if we have brought comfort even to some by patiently bearing with their faults, and encouraged others by giving them, even for an instant, the illusion of recovery.

The Understanding of Good

Is not all the happiness we have known here, and which has given us the strength to live, built up out of the crumbs strewn on our path by certain human beings, borne with patience and with a more understanding love and a larger benevolence?

And is not the richest-seeming human existence sustained in reality by the few luminous threads that bind it to the invisible realities?

The Respect for Love

The law of love is a sacred law given by God to humanity to aid the unfolding of the spiritual, moral and physical being. It responds to humanity's truest and most legitimate aspirations and any violation of it for the sake of sensual joy or under the pretext of virtue, causes irremediable damage to the soul. For here the excess of morality that prevents the development of natural and lawful sentiments is just as blameworthy as the immorality that degrades.

In these days it has become the habit to attach to the idea of love a concealed feeling of guilt. In the eyes of the majority it stands for something stolen, something frivolous. It is a concession made by the spirit to the lower nature in us, admitted, excused in advance, but to which the conscience nevertheless consents with regret and regards with a certain shame. The complacent, malicious smile, always

The Understanding of Good

slightly equivocal, which any mention of love calls forth, proves clearly enough that there is here no possibility of an element of perfection. Like little children who do not know the price of beautiful things, men have made a toy of God's supreme gift. Except in the exalted spirits of poets, of rare idealists and of some women, the respect for love exists no longer. And yet, where that ideal is not venerated, the level of the individual is inevitably lowered. And modern decadence is only one of the obvious results of the general depreciation of the ideal of love.

When a dream of love is about to unfold in the depths of a young heart we hasten to stifle it under ineradicable prejudices, in the name of the primary importance of societal considerations. Many, with a sigh, renounce their dream! Truly it is difficult to distinguish between the elements of reality and of exaltation amidst the tumult of these dawning desires. How shall we justify these yearnings for the already guessed-at truth, in the face of educational influences, worldly example and the obstacles of life? Nine times out of ten the sincere love, the love that ought to raise the

The Respect for Love

thoughts and ennoble the life of the adolescent, is sacrificed to secondary interests. It is clear that reasonable parents cannot always approve the first inclinations of their children's hearts; but, even if they feel obliged to sacrifice them, they should at least guard a respect for the sentiment they have squelched and not depreciate it under the guise of making the parting easier. The moment love is sincere it is worthy of respect, and it is a crime to banish it like a vagrant when it demands a heroic end.

Love sacrificed to accepted duty and offered to God as a fragrance, leaves deep on the soul its breath of the infinite; but the heart from which it has been torn will be forever hardened.

Yet if a man has sinned unconsciously against the laws of love, he may someday regain his original aspirations; but what effort and sorrow will he endure in retracing, among the ruins that life has amassed around him, the path that leads to genuine feelings?

There is perhaps no domain in which falsehood is considered so inconsequential as the dominion of love. On that topic alone is it considered excusable to say what we neither feel nor think. We have outraged love by our

The Understanding of Good

senses, our reason, even by our conscience; and are surprised when, after having so often transgressed the sacred law, life becomes morbid and immeasurably painful.

We seek happiness everywhere — where it seems to be and where it is not — everywhere save in the simple fulfillment of the divine law which a supreme wisdom has given to men for their happiness. For human laws, alas, are very impotent! As many crimes against love are committed in marriage as outside it; with this difference — that the lies of love in marriage are more heinous because they are told under the mantle of duty.

Much could be said on the importance attached to the respect for a tie that is often only the outcome of an odious deception, or that, contracted in error, on the basis of sincere but perhaps unstable sentiments, becomes the prison-house where all the energies of life and all the heart's best hopes are blotted out.

God surely had the welfare and the happiness of men in view when He counseled them to unite in marriage. And deviation from the divine and beneficial thought has its source, like all evils, in egoism. Wherever egoism

The Respect for Love

abdicates, every situation, even one based on error, becomes bearable; everything assumes the place assigned to it. The only true, the only just, useful or supportable marriage, is one based on the respect for mutual liberty.

It would be more equitable to establish marriage, not on the rarely practicable promise of eternal love, but on the vow of a perpetual devotion that extends if necessary even to the sacrifice of love itself. Those who marry unite in order to be a help and not a hindrance to each other. The purpose is always to render happy, whether it be by the gift of oneself or by renunciation.

Nothing can bind save love; nothing severs but indifference; either one loves and is naturally, inevitably faithful; or one does not love and is just as naturally and inevitably unfaithful, even were one in a cloister or banished on a desert island. For faithfulness is a condition of the soul, not a manifestation of our actions; and fidelity can as little be demanded as love.

If, instead of teaching the young what the world allows and forbids, we were to instill in them the desire and the veneration for true love to which all pure hearts aspire, our moral

The Understanding of Good

lectures would become superfluous; for it is the contemplation of and the respect for beauty that preserves us from evil far more surely than the prohibition of the vulgar.

It is true that all are not capable of the highest love; but as we gradually rise above the material, and the moral entity emerges from its corporeal husk, the union of the sexes ought to assume a different character and to respond not only to physical desires but also to the vaster demands of our spiritual beings. For the soul as well as the body has sex and demands union for its completion. Love is not complete and cannot respond to God's thought unless the three aspects of life — body, soul and spirit — participate in it. For one who has recognized and understood this truly, it is not only forbidden but impossible to surrender exclusively to animal instincts.

If, in the organization of our lives and our struggles for progress, we gave the rights of love a larger place, it is probable that men, becoming thereby happier, better and holier, would beget a new generation of strong and thoughtful beings.

The Respect for Love

I have spoken of the interests dictated by reason and by a superficiality in the life of the senses as the most serious enemies of love; there is yet another: false morality.

If the life of the senses ought to be the result and not the purpose of love, it is absurd to regard it as a failing. Every sincere gift is sacred, and the kiss that joins the lips is as pure as the dreams in which souls meet — provided the union be sanctified, not by the authority of human law but by the right of a conscience clear of all fraud. No religious or social consideration can prevail against love, which in itself fulfills all human and divine laws.

The life of the senses is lawful whenever it responds to a natural and sincere feeling, and it is a mistake to attribute to it the disasters that are really due to egoism. It should be justified even in the eyes of the ascetic by the fact that it is part of the moral life and aids its evolution.

Our intellectual, artistic and psychic development really depends in great measure on our emotional life — on our impulses of passion. Deprived of this stimulus, certain characters, gifted with great vitality, would inevitably experience a weakening of soul

The Understanding of Good

and would gradually lose, with the hope of happiness, all desire to live and develop. With them, everything that tends to reduce the life of the senses lowers at the same time their soul's vital force.

If we would grow, we must love; for only the being that inspires such feelings in us can wake the sleeping God in us. The feminine soul asks for strength, breadth, virile independence, while the masculine soul demands for harmonious development the aide of the mystic and psychic affinities of the woman. Nature has assigned to them a supreme end — "to become"; and unable to attain this end alone, they are obliged to seek support from each other. This necessity manifests itself in different degrees according to the type of the individual. There are complex souls that combine all the masculine and feminine qualities necessary for their evolution; but the more pronounced the sex of a soul is, the greater its need of union with another soul to further its own development. Certain men and women might have become saints or produced works of genius had they met the soul destined to complete their being. Failing that union, their powers remained sadly

The Respect for Love

torpid. Others, more fortunate but often less gifted, owe their moral or intellectual victory solely to the encounter with the chosen soul that understood how to arouse their own.

And the soul that has not found its complement continues to seek by instinct and without halt. In youth we seek it in passion.

This is why love, for so many people simply a fortuitous circumstance, is for others life itself. They can only conceive beauty, grasp truth, and realize greatness through the medium of love. In solitude their souls are deprived of light; united, they become transcendent.

If man were sufficiently spiritualized to live in an ideal affection, the end would be gained, and it would be possible without fear of hindering his development, to approve the rigidity of ascetic ideals and uphold the sterile charm of chastity! But as long as we are imprisoned in a body we must accept the consequences of that state and not discourage the well-intentioned by holding up an artificial standard.

Free love is as indispensable as marriage; it has its place in the social organization and can aid individual development, on condition that it be not an expression of egoism but of the

The Understanding of Good

ideal. In whatever form love may present itself, provided only it be true, it fulfills its mission by inspiring us with the highest feelings of which we are capable.

Why attach the condition of virtue to one condition and that of vice to another? Why should free love, any more than marriage, provoke a want of modesty in woman, a lack of dignity and fine feeling; in man a want of austerity, energy and independence? Does one not always remain what one is, in whatever situation one may be placed?

Certain excellent and pure women live entirely outside moral laws, just as others live without real virtue within the strict limit of those same laws. We make our own circumstances; they do not make us, and do not our actions depend on the motive power that has preceded our thoughts? And this power can only oscillate between two poles: God or self — love of the true, or self interest.

In the matter of love, as in every other moral question, truth varies with each individual. Yet I do not mean by free love the sanction of lightness, inconstancy and egoism, the sacrifice of duty to pleasure, nor the right

The Respect for Love

to deceive; but the liberty of self-determination when the exterior tie is only a profanation of the inner treasure of love, and the freedom to love and to give oneself outside law when conscience approves.

Here, as everywhere, there are exceptions — marriages that have no real meaning because they are nothing but a conventional form. Two people, for example, may come together through an error, for a purpose alien to love, and their mistake once realized, they restore to each mutual liberty, since their union was a lie that God could not desire. Does not this moral divorce liberate them as fully as an official divorce, even if for some reason — possibly the education of children — they consider it advisable to remain united outwardly and in a friendly spirit? Other marriages are made through the abuse of confidence, with the sole aim of securing a fortune or a position. Should the victim of this trickery be obliged, if she cannot obtain a divorce, to expiate a moment of naïve faith by the long martyrdom of a life without hope or love?

There are certain things in life which we ought not to accept, because they are beyond

The Understanding of Good

human strength. Sacrilegious marriages, so common in these days, undoubtedly offer a spectacle of the worst sufferings, sufferings which we ought to be able to relieve and to which there should surely be a possible solution far removed from egoism and compatible with the strictest fidelity to an enlightened conscience.

Much is said just now concerning the development of woman; but this development is only possible on a basis of reality, through contact with life and emancipation from all conventional ideas. Not by dreaming, pondering or conjecturing about life can we learn to know it, but by living it! And it is through our collision with reality that we prove our grain.

I believe that many good works for the protection of young girls and women would be superfluous if from the start the education of women were carried on *in* life and *by* life. Limited to a region so narrow and artificial, woman, and particularly the woman of the more educated classes, finds it impossible to develop her personality or gain the means of making herself respected. Ignorant of the world surrounding her and of the world within her which she has never learned to know and to

The Respect for Love

control, she is from the outset at the mercy of all dangers.

In order to know life it is not necessary to condone vice but simply to walk with eyes open and alert, to see what is taking place and judge what is best to take or to leave, to follow or avoid.

As long as woman leads a fictitious life she must remain incomplete; but as soon as she can live naturally and truly amidst all that life holds of the beautiful, good and true, she will attain her full stature and become a useful instrument in the evolution of humanity. She, rather than man, being destined to prepare men for life, ought surely to know it so that she may be not only the nurse and the servant but also the friend and counselor of her children. For only experience can influence. The most devoted son, feeling that his mother is ignorant of life, cannot follow her counsels, for he will find them artificial and worthless. He will inevitably suspect her of preaching virtue to him in order to conform to usage, or from a sense of duty, and will think in spite of himself: "Does she know what I know, see what I see; has she struggled as I struggle?" By preference he will

The Understanding of Good

turn to the counsels of his comrades who are as lacking in wisdom as he is himself, but who at least understand his longings and know what life is.

The ignorance of life in which woman is intentionally kept, under the pretext of preserving her chastity, but in reality to guard by egoism that which constitutes her chief charm to many men, is the principal cause not only of her unhappiness but often also of her lack of purity; for purity, like all the virtues, is only acquired by conflict. Certain beings are purer than others because, having been in conflict with evil, they have suffered more for the sake of good. A truly pure life is one that, fully cognizant of reality, has known how to surmount it.

If love, given to man for his happiness, has too often been the cause of his sorrow, it is not love we should accuse but the deviation from love. Between the man and woman who love there exists nearly always a misapprehension that arises from their mutual ignorance of each other's aspirations. And it is this misunderstanding that finally separates them.

The Respect for Love

I am not speaking of the vulgar love that only seeks its own satisfaction, but of the genuine feeling which, even when preoccupied with the happiness of the loved being, only too often causes it sorrow.

In love, man makes the mistake of not truly trying to understand the soul of woman; he seeks in her the mystery that caresses the sensuous side of his nature rather than the intelligence that would have rendered her capable of satisfying his heart. Or he turns woman into an instrument of pleasure and grovels at her feet, depriving himself of the best she has to give him. Or he adores her as a goddess and expects her to quench his endless thirst. Unable to satiate his soul, she cannot be content merely to gratify his appetites; but what man nearly always forgets is this: that woman, being a human creature animated by the same feelings and prey to the same difficulties as himself, has a right to the same conditions of life, and cannot fulfill her mission unless her veritable self is recognized and appealed to. If in our day woman has seen herself forced to seek in the activity of public work an outlet for faculties often foreign to her intrinsic nature,

The Understanding of Good

it is because she can no longer consecrate her natural qualities to man; she has been obliged to put away some of her womanliness because it has not met with understanding. Man looks for repose and distraction in love; woman seeks in it the unfolding of her being.

Woman's mistake in the realm of love is the desire to captivate man — also a form of egoism, though differing from masculine egoism. She believes that the love which suffices for her needs will equally suffice for man; she thus seeks to fit him into her own groove, forgetting to respect in him the aspirations outside and beyond love, and ignoring his right to gratify them. She lacks simplicity and candor in not recognizing the moment when she should put off the woman and become the friend.

And thus the ignorance of man has deprived woman of the best that love has to give; and the paltriness of woman has driven man away from it; in her obstinate desire to keep him her slave, she has incited him to seek his freedom in pleasure.

If man would learn to have a better understanding of love, and woman to depend less on it, the law of God, which has created

The Respect for Love

man and woman to complete each other, would be accomplished. For no science, no ambition, no joy can replace that marvelous unfolding which true love brings to the soul.

Grace and Inspiration

Grace is to the believer what inspiration is to the artist; it is an unknown force which, added momentarily to our nature, renders it capable of something which until then was impossible. As soon as this divine breath stirs us, we become the instruments of a superhuman power that dominates us for the purposes of an unknown end, far beyond our comprehension.

The intervention of grace has been attributed to the degree of our piety, as that of inspiration to certain physical dispositions, produced by the use of alcohol, the position of the body, or atmospheric influences. But in reality it comes to the most diverse individuals, quite apart from their capacities or their merits. As certain criminals have been known to realize the enormity of their crime at the instant of raising their murderous weapon, and certain persons of great mediocrity have been

The Understanding of Good

capable under a sudden luminous impulsion of producing great works of art, so there have been saints who never felt the joys of the Holy Spirit, and men of genius who never achieved the materialization of their vision.

Here it would seem, as in everything else, that God has willed to differentiate between the free gift and the earned wage, so that man should always remain dependent on the divine and be preserved from the mercenary spirit as well as from all false pride. It is perfectly just that in our state of incomplete development we should be subject to laws we must accept without being able to understand. The most advanced among us feel that the highest beauty lies in the inexplicable, and that the most noble movement of man is the act of faith by which he accepts this mystery.

Detachment

As we advance along the path of life and realize more clearly the inadequacy of even the best things to satisfy the yearnings of our soul, we come to look on worldly advantages with greater indifference; we pursue them with a lagging step and suffer less keenly and more briefly from their loss. Is there actually a lessening of life's force? Not so, but a simple transference to the life that is seeking a higher level.

How naturally we cease to desire the object of our dreams when we perceive a higher object, even should this bring us less rapture through the fact of its being invisible and indefinable; to be calmer is not necessarily to be less vital. In the tranquility of the philosopher, watching the current of life on which he no longer depends, there is quite as much fervor and hope as in the tumultuous passion of the adolescent.

Our vain efforts toward the desired object have exhausted our strength but they have

The Understanding of Good

added to our real value; we feel less need of a personal happiness and understand more clearly the disinterested joy which gives to the soul all that is beautiful, good and true on earth.

We continue to desire tangible happiness, but we are able to await it in quietude because the higher ideal that has come into being within us has taught us to depend on it no longer.

To detach oneself does not mean a diminished capacity for love, but the renunciation of that love which is of no real worth. Deliberate detachment is an error: one cannot detach oneself by an effort of will; on the contrary, the more one longs to renounce something the more one will cling to it. Voluntary detachment is merely a falsehood to oneself which, sooner or later, betrayed nature will avenge. Only a natural detachment, the logical consequence of what we have undergone, can be effective. There is no danger that this gradual detachment will shatter our vital strength, because it adjusts in accordance with our spiritual progress.

We ought never to meet events with fixed ideas but rather let them come to us bringing their own lessons of truth. We can only judge

Detachment

things after and not before we have experienced them. Those who remain rigid in the armor of their beliefs are incapable of progress, for truth is not in precept but in practice. The more supple we remain in the molding hand of destiny, the more perfect will be the form which the mysterious sculptor can impress on us.

It is of little use to say to a young creature in love with life that the good things of the world will not be able to satisfy his heart; he will not believe you. And perhaps, even, he ought not to believe you, for he would be lying to himself if he accepted a truth without having first proved it. Far better is it that all should taste the delights of the world, even at the cost of a temporary deterioration, if only thereby to gain the conviction of their insufficiency; for only then will they be able to surrender themselves free-heartedly and without regret to the invisible.

Nor is it well to encourage the practice of spirituality in the young — and how many remain children for the greater part of their lives! It is enough that they should see spiritual realities made living around them in order that

The Understanding of Good

they may drink of that divine cup when their hour shall come.

Let us be careful not to force nature; it is she who is truly wise and who will herself plan the whole course of our development. Short of the existence of diseased tendencies or proclivities dangerous to public welfare, we can safely leave a human creature to the guidance of his own nature: it will perhaps lead him along many a rough path but with certainty toward the goal assigned to him by fate. Our zeal is nearly always misplaced; in its efforts to reform or to hinder evil, it puts itself in opposition to that experience which each must make for himself, sooner or later, if he is finally to gain his full moral stature.

The last fetter from which woman frees herself is passion, for her false status in life often deprives her of direct contact with this force. Our worst enemies are always those whom we cannot fight face to face, because they only reveal themselves to us shadowed in the veil of dreams.

It is easy to renounce what one has once possessed, but we continue to long for that from which we have been debarred. Nature knows

Detachment

instinctively that she cannot be complete unless all the possibilities that are in her have been employed, potentialities so varied and so vast that a single existence seems utterly inadequate for their full development.

Detachment is often the result of life's defeat; independence is always a victory over life.

Happiness! Love! Ideal! Home! All that our soul has yearned for, all that life has denied us! To behold you we have climbed the arid slopes, to reach you we have borne all storms and tempests. It is because we believed that you were hidden in the vast Unknown, even as we felt you stirring in our heart, that we had the strength to struggle onward to the present hour.

Happiness! Love! Ideal! Home! We shall never possess you, but from afar, oh, so far! We can still discern you.

When the evening hour shall come and find us sitting on the threshold of our ruined habitation, we shall at last understand that the greatest earthly felicity leads but to the frontiers of heaven, and that we must die leaving the Rose of Canaan ungathered; and at last, through our tears, we shall softly smile; we shall know that the goal is reached. For the end

The Understanding of Good

was not that our hands should grasp but that our eyes might learn to see.

The Quiet Force

As soon as a few stray gleams penetrate the forest, we understand its marvelous beauty; and the soul has need of emotion, joy and transcendence to enable it to realize its own immortal grandeur; but when night falls it seems to us as if all growth has ceased.

And yet do we really owe our progress to the conquests of our thought and our faith? Is there not a force more real, more stable, in the depths of our soul, which stands for our true greatness and on which alone we truly lean?

Its presence is a mystery; we feel its workings yet know not whence it comes or how it exists in us. Called forth by our will, it yet eludes our action and lives outside the circle of our emotions. It is as though its essence were other and had its source elsewhere. Stored up by our efforts, as the grains of sand on the ocean-bed that mount until they become

The Understanding of Good

venerable rocks, we yet know that this force is not produced by us; and though we may rely on it, we do so only because we believe in a supreme justice.

In the hour of a troubled conscience, it is present — an unseen warden. If our foot slips, a smile meets us. When our courage fails, there is support at hand. It seems as if all that passes in our conscious being has little meaning for it, scarcely concerns it, being only the breeze that ruffles the surface of the waters but does not divert the current.

This force rests in us as a precious possession, the power and lasting value of which a secret voice ensures. Though it is in no way dependent on our impulses or actions, all our life depends on it; for it is the force that in all our victories or defeats ceases not to urge us forward; and it is surely because we count on this mysterious asset that even in the vortex of our most ignominious failures we will not surrender, but still push on though all our strength is spent. This force that cannot be born of our will has need, nevertheless, of our endeavors.

As there are sins which do not alter the value of our soul, so there are honest virtues

The Quiet Force

that do not augment our true worth. If our virtues are to become immortal and add a ray to our divine aura, the effort that has produced them must emanate from the depths of our soul.

Our inner life embraces different regions: here it is of stirring grandeur, there all is smiling peace; but most men fear to venture themselves along the sinister paths that lead to the abyss, or to stray in the solitude of the summits; they merely parade their emotions on the highways and in the level glades. These will never know the immortal force, for only that which has passed through death can reach life.

Our soul comes to resemble what it most looks upon, and if at a decisive hour it has had the courage to gaze on something greater than itself it will have grown to that same greatness.

And it is only in the regions of the tragic, the solemn, the imposing and the marvelous that we can acquire those superhuman qualities that raise us above all temporal happenings.

This quiet force renders us independent of the circumstances of life by giving us the power to discern and to separate our higher from our lower self. Though still remaining, by

The Understanding of Good

reason of our emotional nature, at the mercy of events, we find in our immortal being a shelter from their attacks.

And loss follows a sort of dividing, as it were, of our personality, one part of which struggles in the throes of reality, while the other frees itself and looks on from the region of a higher truth. We shall still suffer, but the part of us that suffers is less intimately *ourself.* It seems as if this best of our self, removed from strife, no longer shares so keenly in the vicissitudes of its unfortunate brother: his cries cause it less anguish, his defeats no longer drive it to despair; it would wish him to be gay, but only as one wishes happiness to a stranger, when one's own interest is not at stake. It is, after all, of small importance if his inferior self is victor or vanquished in this strange crisis we call life, for how can real tragedy touch a being whose humiliation is transient and whose triumph is ephemeral? Immersed in life, we still have the power at any moment to render it objective; independent of it, we can be strong.

This force gives us the mastery over events. The weak flee from the powers that surround them and remain eternally beneath

The Quiet Force

their sway; the strong, on the contrary, allow them to affront them with all their violence, risking their crushing impact, and fight them face to face in a faithful and decisive combat; for we can only become independent of things on which we have once depended, and masters of that which we have overcome.

The greatest power of man is not that which can conquer but that which can endure; the real hero is not he who waves the flag of victory in triumph but he who, suffering, bears the ignominy of defeat; for it means less to overcome outward obstacles than to steadfastly conquer those within ourselves.

This force that fights step by step, doggedly till it drops, that struggles without asking why, expecting no reward, that fights for fighting's sake, from necessity, from duty, perhaps from habit, and which we call endurance, is the sign in man of the supreme victory.

The weak resign themselves; the superficial find consolation; those who are not sincere deceive themselves and so find a cure for their ills; only those who have the courage to continue suffer always, and their suffering is their sanction. Thus the continuance of pain,

The Understanding of Good

too often looked upon as a punishment or a weakness, may really spring from high merit and testify to the highest strength.

It may be that I no longer feel the courage to hold out a hand to my brother, or to make another step along life's path; but if the force is in me it will give my infirmity such strength that my brother will be fortified by my mere proximity, and I, in spite of my weakness, shall not cease to climb toward the summit.

He who is strong no longer disappoints his brothers; true to himself, he can be true to others. His conduct will always be consistent for all that he gives forth — feelings, words, deeds — will emanate from the indestructible center of his real being. He can enjoy the tranquil assurance of well-earned value, the proved certainty of a steady advance and the gentle calm of a quiet conscience.

Certainty

No more oppression under the bondage of a burdensome law, no more ceaseless labor toward an artificial ideal; a trusting surrender to free development is now the fulfilling of the law. The divine germ has sprouted and has transformed all things.

To vibrate, to accept, to expand — this is the new duty; to give oneself as one is, to let life meet us as it really is, to live for the moment and extract from each moment all that it holds of truth, beauty and goodness, without misgivings or concealed motives, without vain questioning, in the spontaneous desire of life, in childlike purity of heart; to be able to be oneself, to dare to be happy; and at last allow one's soul to spread its wings and in a natural and impulsive ardor rise up to God.

To will no more — for to will is to impose a direction on destiny — but to let ourselves be led where fate will lead us, even were the path

The Understanding of Good

not the one we desired; for life is everywhere, happiness in all things, it is we who create them.

To pass beyond the zone of tribulation and the sickness of scruples; to be capable of facing all, free to accept all; to have faith in one's own heart and to give as the heart dictates; for the sincere heart is also pure.

He who has understood these things no longer lives in the satisfaction of a duty accomplished or in the uncertain hope of a realized dream, but in the immortal richness of his intimate experiences. The unfolding of his true humanity, in which he takes part as at the unrolling of a miraculous scene, brings him intense emotions; it is an absorbing interest which he carries everywhere he goes and which is renewed and enriched at every contact with life. His life will never more be bare of heroism, or his soul deprived of noble impulses, for his feelings will vibrate in unison with the Infinite, and the drama of his life will be completed in Eternity.

The wise man is he who can draw truth from his soul and who has no need of the approval of an established order to enable him to follow it; who likewise can believe in God

Certainty

without being shown a ready-made Divinity. He respects all things because he understands the compass of truth, but he remains himself because he believes that his individual voice has its appointed views equally with that of others. The wise man does not seek the support of others; he knows that their love is a blessing on which he must not count and that an hour of solitude is worth more than the best counsels. As a king in his kingdom he walks alone in his strength — alone, but linked to all that is great, beautiful and true in the universe.

The wise man does not consider how to give, he only asks to *be*, knowing that the results he produces will always be in proportion to his worth, and that no one can fill his brother's lamp with oil.

Desires, regrets, joys, sorrows — why should he fear them? Are they not those who, stirring his soul, cause it to live? Above all movement there is contemplation, eternal certainty — the Beyond of good and evil, the Infinite, the changeless Home.

The wise man is he who knows how to enjoy all things but *needs* nothing, who can lose all and yet remain rich. Earth keeps all her beauty

The Understanding of Good

for him; but her beauty's richest endowment lies in the intuition of his own discerning gaze. Heaven is always desirable, but it means more to him to know he is worthy of it than to enjoy it, even could he never find it within his reach. He has learned to create within himself all he has need of, all he had vainly searched for outside. He can only say to the ray that falls across his path: "Your light has shed a glow on my hearth as it passed; withdrawing, the darkness you leave behind cannot dim any part of its brightness. In my youth I lived by what intoxicates, and languished in the wearisome; now that I have attained wisdom I no longer live by what I feel but by what I can be; and Beauty, Happiness, Love need no longer knock at my door to tell me I am joyful. It is enough for me to know that they sometimes pass my way.

Heaven for the wise man is not a reward to come but the liberation of the sovereign soul that can overcome all things. The wise man is benevolent toward all his fellows; he no longer fears their weapons, he understands all their misfortunes. Only the wise man and the little child can smile with impunity at the

Certainty

movements of life's wheel: the one because he knows nothing, the other because he knows that all is nothing.

The wise man is he who moves among men but has his dwelling on the mountain; and that dwelling is as immovable as the stars in the firmament.

For those who have had the courage to sacrifice their happiness, their rest, their ideal and their religion in order to obey the voice of God in their hearts, there remains a home even were they in the desert; for they have felt that at the bottom of this void something lives, something more real than their firmest faith, their pious hopes, more intimate than the secret of their thoughts, the beating of their hearts; something more marvelous than the rapture of their young happiness; something so vast that it embraces all their aspirations, so high that no happenings can reach it.

It is a respite, an inner shelter, a never-changing treasure whose presence, once realized, floods our soul with joy and transports it beyond all human limits; carrying it into the Infinite, the Perfect.

The Understanding of Good

It is an immortal temple rising in the midst of all that is transient, which abides when all else is gone, which promises us the continuance of that which we are and the plenitude of that which we shall one day be!

How mysterious is this Temple! Its stones are our stored sorrows — but an unknown master has built them up. Our efforts have pierced the walls — but an invisible hand has let in the light. Our faith has built the steps — but across the threshold a silent angel has led us.

Truly, Oh God, we are kings in this temple — but the crown was placed upon our brow by Thee alone!

Gleam of Light Press is dedicated to the inner life that is so often neglected in our everyday lives. We are dedicated to the kind of reading that awakens souls, lifts spirits, and enriches lives. Our plan is to grow slowly and thoughtfully, to publish a few select books that we feel are important and also to recommend other great finds. We hope you will check in with us occasionally, pursue some of our offerings, and share your ideas with us.

Gleam of Light Press, LLC
P.O. Box 42
Lakeland, Michigan 48143 USA
GleamOfLightPress.com